Bloody Revenge

BLOODY REVENGE

Emotions, Nationalism, and War

THOMAS J. SCHEFF

AN AUTHORS GUILD BACKINPRINT.COM EDITION

Bloody Revenge
Emotions, Nationalism and War
All Rights Reserved © 1994, 2000 by Thomas J. Scheff

AN AUTHORS GUILD BACKINPRINT.COM EDITION

Published by iUniverse.com, Inc.

For information address:
iUniverse.com, Inc.
620 North 48th Street, Suite 201
Lincoln, NE 68504-3467
www.iuniverse.com

Originally published by Winston-Derek Publishers, Inc.

ISBN: 0-595-13110-7

Printed in the United States of America

To all innocent victims of humiliated fury

Vilna, 1924. My Aunt Rachel is telling the fortune of my Uncle Hym and my Grandfather Lazar Heifetz. She did not foresee what fate would befall them seventeen years later.

Contents

Part Two: APPLICATIONS

Part Three: CONCLUSION

Figures

Acknowledgments

I am indebted to many persons for help during the writing of this book. Rodney Beaulieu, Joan Murdoch, and Mark Schildhauer provided expert suggestions on word processing and printing. Christine Allen organized miscellaneous clerical support and supplied wisecracks in the face of my unending demands. Advice on Chapter 4, for me the most difficult part, was rendered by John Braithwaite, Robin Evans, Gabrielle Hoffman, and Robert Marsh. Edward Muir read the first four chapters, and Nancy Carlston, Eric Dunning, Louis Kriesberg, Nicholas Tavuchis, and an anonymous Westview Press reviewer read a draft of the whole book. Randall Collins and Suzanne Retzinger provided comments, support, and encouragement during the lengthy process of revision. The feedback that I got from these readers has helped me immeasurably in writing this book.

Thomas J. Scheff

Introduction

This book proposes a theory of protracted conflict and a method appropriate to such a theory. Since my approach departs from many of the conventions current in the human sciences, a preliminary sketch of premises may help orient the reader.

The argument is self-contained; knowledge of other sources is not required. Inevitably, however, the present statement depends on earlier work by myself, Retzinger (my wife), and others. The general approach advances the argument offered earlier in *Microsociology* (Scheff, 1990). The specifics of the theory and method closely follow prior work by Retzinger (1991). Another book (Scheff and Retzinger, 1991) was a rehearsal for the kind of micro-macro analysis I attempt here. A brief outline of the main issues addressed in these prior volumes provides a framework for the present approach.

Theory

The Social Bond

Retzinger and I propose that earlier work in many fields has established the crucial importance of the *social bond* in human behavior. This conception gives rise to an approach to conflict that focuses on the relationships between individuals and between groups. Although the concept of a relationship is so primitive, it has never been adequately explicated in the human sciences.

As in our earlier work, this book specifies key aspects of interpersonal and collective relationships. I assume that the social bond is a real and palpable phenomenon and that in every type of human contact it is being either *built, maintained, repaired, or damaged*. In this context, we see alienation or damaged bonds as a basic cause of destructive conflict.

Our preliminary definition of a secure bond involves what I have called "attunement" (Scheff, 1990). Persons (and groups) who understand each other both cognitively and emotionally are apt to trust and cooperate. Even when they are in competition or conflict, there are clear boundaries and limits. There is a realization that even in a state of conflict, they are ultimately all in the same boat. Limited wars are a product of bond networks within and between disputants in which attunement prevails over misunderstanding.

By the same token, unlimited destruction is a product of broken bonds. One of Simmel's many insights implies as much: "The deepest hatred grows out of broken love. ... Here separation does not follow from conflict, but, on the contrary, conflict from separation" (1955, p. 47). In a sense, this book and our three earlier ones are attempts to unpack Simmel's statement, which is uncannily complex in that it suggests interrelations among several crucial concepts: hatred, broken love, separation, and conflict. Note also the implication of a spiral: how separation leads to conflict, and conflict in turn leads to further separation, ad infinitum. Our main effort has been to show how separation and the spiral of separation and conflict can be detected in actual discourse. Surprisingly, the four books en masse have barely scratched the surface of the implications of Simmel's comment.

In our definition, alienation involves a lack of understanding or a misunderstanding, either cognitively or emotionally. As the subsequent chapters will show, there were gross misunderstandings between the disputants prior to the outbreak of World War I. Both sides, for example, thought themselves so much stronger than the other that they predicted a war would be a frolic. The lack of understanding in this case led to an unnecessarily quick resort to war.

At the onset of the World War II, the lack of understanding had the opposite result. The Allies' misconceptions about Germany's intentions and its determination to fight led them to delay going to war for much longer than necessary. An Allied declaration of war at the time of the German incursion into the Sudetenland would have resulted in a constructive conflict since the German military was weak at the time, and, more importantly, support for Hitler in Germany was not yet consolidated. My approach seeks to explain *irrational* management of disputes, whether they involve fighting or not.

Our exact formulation of the relational cause of destructive conflict concerns the state of bonds both within and between nations. We propose that a certain state of bondlessness has lethal implications: We call it "bimodal alienation." This state involves isolation between nations and engulfment within them. In our formulation, engulfment is the kind of blind loyalty and conformity that arise when persons deny important parts of themselves. Chapter 1 provides an example. One reason that Rosie and James are discussing divorce is that both hide and deny their feelings of anger and shame. Engulfment means alienation from *self,* just as isolation means alienation from others.

Destructive wars require not only isolation between nations but also engulfment within: blind loyalty that overrides reason and dissent. A well-known example occurred in the discussions before the Bay of Pigs disaster. We now know that one of President Kennedy's most trusted advisers, Ball, was intensely opposed to the invasion, but he withheld his dissenting opinion. It would be of great interest to investigate his bond network at this time. My hypothesis is that none of his bonds was secure, either in his professional or personal life. Otherwise he would have spoken up, even in the face of a seemingly unified array of all the other advisers.

Our emphasis on the social bond clashes with the realist approach, which dominates current theories of conflict. In this viewpoint, disputes between persons and between groups are grounded in conflicts of material interests. Since the state of the bond is not immediately evident in behavior but must be inferred, our approach also clashes with the behaviorist orientation, which dominates most current research in the human sciences.

We assume that human beings are so intelligent that they are always capable of finding a *compromise* between conflicting interests that is mutually rewarding, or at least minimally damaging, to both parties. Given this premise, we argue that protracted conflict is always a product of relationships issues that go unacknowledged by both sides. One or both sides have been humiliated or threatened in such a way as to disturb fundamental human bonds, but this disturbance is not acknowledged. Unacknowledged threats to the bond and shame go hand in hand; they set the stage for cycles of insult, humiliation, and revenge. In what Goffman (1967) called "character contests," *any* issue can become a *causus belli.*

Material interests figure as part of our equation of conflict. They are the "topics" that dominate discourse between and within groups in conflict. Relationship talk, which contrasts with topic talk, comprises the thoughts and feelings of the disputants, especially those directed toward each other. Since disputants avoid relationship issues in favor of topics, they are unable to resolve the threats to the bond.

These threats give rise to violent emotions, such as shame and rage, and thereby set the stage for unending and unproductive conflict. This tableau is clearly illustrated in the marital dispute analyzed in the first chapter. Rosie and James talk only about the airplane they own, not about the feelings of rejection that are threatening their marriage. They were entrapped in unproductive conflict about topics until relationship issues were brought out into the open.

Pride and Shame

A key aspect of the bond between persons and between groups is the emotions of pride and shame. We have argued in our earlier work that pride generates and signals a secure bond, just as shame generates and signals a threatened bond. For this reason, these two emotions have a unique status relative to social relationships. They are the emotional facets of a relationship, just as the bond is the relational aspect of pride and shame. These emotions are one side of a coin; the bond is the other. They are so intricately related that strict separation between them is imposed by the limitations of the English language. Our language is deficient in precise, complex, and subtle words describing emotional and relational states.

Pride and shame play a central role in both our theory and method. In the theory, the social and psychological management of shame determines cooperation or conflict, peace or war. Shame is a basic cause of the escalation of conflict. When not acknowledged, shame leads directly to anger, insult, and aggression. Lewis (1971), in her magnum opus, showed that patient hostility toward the therapist was always preceded by unacknowledged shame. However, Lewis did not set out to demonstrate this point. Her instances were scattered throughout hundreds of shame episodes of all kinds. It takes a careful reading to see that she has demonstrated her idea that there is "a strong affinity between shame and anger."

Retzinger's (1991) demonstration of a similar proposition is much more forceful. Her study was focused on the proposition that *unacknowledged shame causes angry escalation* in marital disputes. She showed that shame cues always preceded anger and escalation in every one of the hundreds of episodes she examined, with no exceptions.

Retzinger demonstrated that for the four couples she studied, unacknowledged shame was a *sufficient* condition for the escalation of disputes. She did not, however, establish shame as a *necessary* condition. It is possible that other emotions, such as fear, can also cause escalation. Fear seems to be sufficient to cause panic behavior. It is conceivable that escalation of conflict can be generated by panics of fear as well as by shame. Because of the limitations of our data and of the techniques for detecting fear cues, we have not eliminated the possibility that fear may play a role in causing conflict.

In the method we use, indicators of pride and shame provide an instant readout of the state of the bond. By detecting cues to these emotions, we can assess the "temperature" of a relationship in every moment. In the chapters on Franco-German conflict, I use French poems, novels, and Hitler's writings and speeches to assess the state of the bond. As is the case with our focus on social bonds, our emphasis on emotions also departs from most current approaches to conflict, which emphasize the material and behavioral causes of conflict.

Method

Parts and Wholes

In my earlier volume (Scheff, 1990) I specify a general approach to theory and method that I call "part/whole." This approach places equal emphasis on the smallest parts of a social system, the words and gestures in discourse, and the largest wholes, the institutions that exist within and between nations. In this view, understanding human behavior depends on rapid movement between the parts and wholes, interpreting each in terms of the other.

My approach is similar to what is called morphology in botany, the study of the structure and function of plants. This approach looks at a single specimen in order to understand the species as well as studying the species in order to understand the specimen. To understand how a single specimen works requires a quite detailed microscopic examination of all its details, no matter how small. Otherwise those details that are needed in explanation might be left out. Darwin's theory of evolution grew out of his observations of extremely small variations in the appearance of species living in separate regions. Had his method been more focused and "rigorous" (by current standards) in the form of an experiment or survey, he probably would have ignored these tiny details.

Applying this method to the human sphere, I have focused on single concrete episodes of behavior: the inception of a marital quarrel at the interpersonal level, two world wars at the international level. I emphasize a "bottom-up" strategy, starting with a detailed examination of single events, as well as a "top-down" strategy, a bird's-eye view of many events in terms of abstract concepts. Part/whole reasoning requires that both strategies be used in conjunction.

In this approach, the smallest unit of sociation is the *exchange,* an utterance by one party and the response to it by the other party. As will be seen, social structure and emotion are hidden largely in the smallest parts of an exchange, the words, gestures, and details of the interpersonal and historical context. In face-to-face quarrels between persons, the sources of irrational conflict seem to be located, for the most part, in nonverbal elements, in the paralinguistic and kinesic features of discourse. In exchanges that are entirely verbal, as in poems, novels, and correspondence between heads of state, although there are no nonverbal elements, the manner of verbal expression is still of great importance as a cue to social structure and emotion. (See particularly the analysis of the telegrams by the czar of Russia to the kaiser of Germany in Chapter 4.)

Of equal importance in understanding conflict is what is *not* said but could have been said (I call these imagined statements *hypotheticals*). In some ways the most important aspect of the exchanges between the heads of state before the declaration of war in 1914 was not what was said but was might have been said but was not. For example, the demands that Austria made on Serbia in the crisis following the assassination of the Archduke Ferdinand were so massive and contemptuous as to be humiliating. Although diplomats spoke among themselves of this feature, it was never openly discussed by representatives of the major disputants. In Chapter 6 I examine two hypotheticals: a summit meeting among representatives of the six major disputants to try avoiding war and, as one of the items that might have been considered in such a meeting, the language of the Austrian ultimatum.

Hypotheticals may be extraordinarily important for the researcher because they allow distancing from the actual historical situation. Understanding what *could* have happened but did not can help the researcher understand what *did* happen. In my point of view, the disputants in destructive conflict are deeply entrapped in a system in which impediments to headlong catastrophe have been removed. The more knowledgeable the researcher becomes about the details of a conflict, the more identified he or she becomes with one or the other disputant, the greater is the temptation to enter the same trap in which the disputants were caught. The long-term and immediate proposals for conciliation in Chapter 6, even if they prove to be of little value for promoting peace between nations, can serve as prods to the researcher's imagination.

Hypotheticals help researchers escape the actual historical traps. As Peirce ([1908] 1955) argued, scientific work depends on *abduction*, parity between observation and imagination. Hypothetical episodes can be as important as actual ones and should be treated with the same attention to details of verbal and nonverbal communication.

Important as the details of discourse are, they are all but meaningless without an understanding of the context in which they occur. To determine the meaning of messages of any kind, researchers need to know quite a lot about the situation of which such messages are a part. The understanding of context is particularly important in formal messages since they leave so much unsaid. It is for this reason that more of the chapters on the two world wars are devoted to the historical context than to the actual messages I examine. I use the part/whole method to move back and forth between the details of a message and the context in which it occurs.

Part/whole analysis strongly departs from the convention of specialization by discipline that currently dominates the human sciences. My analysis of the inception of World War I and of Hitler's appeal to the Germans calls equally upon four different disciplines: history, political science, linguistics (discourse analysis), and the sociology of emotions.

Cues to Emotion

In social interaction persons seldom say what emotions they are experiencing. In order to interpret their emotions, we note outer cues to their inner state. If someone is yelling and shaking a fist, one usually decides that he or she is angry, even if this emotion is not put into words.

We use the process of abduction in making inferences about emotions. That is, we move rapidly back and forth between observation and imagination. Observing my friend's gestures of yelling and fist waving, I imagine that he is angry. I then *search* for confirming evidence in the immediate and extended context (Scheff, 1990). For example, drawing upon my knowledge of our relationship, I begin to imagine reasons for his anger. Selecting the reason that seems most likely—say, the money that I owe him, which is overdue—I might go on to question him about it, trying to move the discourse to the level of words. For negotiation and compromise, symbolic communication is far superior to gestural conversation, since the former can range far and wide over the entire spectrum of the dispute and its possible outcomes, escaping in this way from the emotion traps I discuss in this book.

The process of abduction is used with regard not only to emotions but also to all purposive human activity. For example, abduction is every bit as important in understanding verbal messages in ordinary language as it is in nonverbal ones. In all natural human languages (excepting artificial ones, such as mathematical and programming languages), every word used is a more or less ambiguous token whose exact meaning can be determined only in context.

The personal pronouns are an obvious example. They are blank checks whose value can be filled in only by context: the meaning of you, him, there, etc. is determined entirely by the accompanying verbal and nonverbal elements. A close examination of any instance of natural language shows that all language components are so ambiguous as to be understandable only in context (Scheff, 1990).

There is one great difference, however, between verbal and nonverbal language. The meaning of words has been partly institutionalized in the form of dictionaries. Although formal definitions of words are only crude and ambiguous approximations, they provide hints and boundaries to meaning and serve as guides for adjudicating disputes about meaning.

At this point in the study of emotions, researchers do not have adequate dictionaries of cues to meaning. It is for this reason that Retzinger's (1991) list of cues to anger and shame are important for this book (Retzinger's cue summary can be found in the Appendix). She drew together cues to anger and shame from earlier specialized studies by other researchers.

The earlier studies were specialized either by emotion or by type of cue (verbal, paralinguistic, or kinesic). For example, Gottschalk et al. (1969) included cue lists for shame, anger, anxiety, and many other emotions but were concerned only with verbal cues. Retzinger provided the first comprehensive procedure for detecting shame and anger cues.

My analysis of shame and anger in social interaction is based on Retzinger's approach. I use her entire list of cues in my analysis of the marital quarrel in Chapter 1. Even with purely verbal texts, in my analysis of French poems and novels, the messages between heads of state before World War I, and Hitler's writings and speeches, I still depend on the coding system devised by Retzinger.

This dependence on a procedure for coding shame and anger cues is both a strength and limitation of my analysis. On the one hand, it allows for a systematic approach to the interpretation of meaning, a new development in interpretive studies. On the other hand, it limits my analysis to only two emotions: anger and shame. It is possible that other emotions also figure in destructive conflict.

One emotion already mentioned, fear, has been suggested by other analysts as a possible causal agent in conflict. For example, Gaylin (1984) suggested that fear and shame are equally involved in producing rage. Although his argument is plausible, it is different in kind from the one I make in this book. Gaylin included descriptions of several concrete episodes but did not even consider the possibility that they needed to be analyzed in a systematic way. His argument was entirely conceptual and undocumented. He did not provide a prima facie case for fear as a cause of conflict, as Retzinger (1991) did for shame.

My argument, unlike Gaylin's, arises from the systematic analysis of discourse. The fact that this argument is systematic and empirical does not guarantee that it is true, of course. But it does expose theory and method to criticism and modification. Indeed, I learn something new both about my theory and Rosie and James each time I or my students analyze their discourse. My interest in my subjects is forever renewed by collisions between an explicit theory and immovable data. I do not think a similar statement can be made about Gaylin's analysis or the many others similar to it. Like Gaylin, most discussions of emotion use undefined terms in a casual way, with little or no documentation for their assertions.

But my approach, even though the theory is explicit and the method is systematic, involves a cost as well as a benefit. The cost is that my approach has not eliminated the possibility that other emotions, such as fear (and casting a much wider net, anxiety) can also generate conflict, as will be further discussed in Chapter 6.

Reliability and Validity

The study of the exact meaning of texts falls under many headings, such as semiotics and hermeneutics. Although there is an enormous literature on this topic, even its most zealous proponents do not claim that interpretation can ever be anything but an art, something largely subjective.

In contrast to prevailing opinion, I earlier proposed an approach (Scheff, 1990) to the objective interpretations of texts. Here I recapitulate the argument only in brief. It applies only to verbatim texts, which herein are of two kinds: the transcript of the quarrel between Rosie and James (Chapter 1) and its accompanying videotape and verbal texts (stanzas of poems, diplomatic exchanges immediately prior to the beginning of World War I, and Hitler's writings and speeches) (Chapters 4 and 5).

My approach to interpreting verbatim texts has two components. First the specific techniques used in interpretation must be made explicit. Second, the entire text must accompany the research report or be available to readers, either in the historical record or, in the case of audio- and videotapes, upon request to the researcher. The texts interpreted in Chapters 4 and 5 are part of the historical record. The verbatim text that is the basis for Chapter 1 is available in part from the original researcher (as will be specified).

I have previously argued (Scheff, 1990) that if these two conditions are met (interpretive procedures are clearly specified, and the verbatim texts are available), then the resulting interpretation has a reliability-validity level that is competitive with other objective procedures in the human sciences.

The explicit presentation of the technique of interpretation allows the reader to judge and criticize its relevance to the research undertaken, its validity. And the inclusion of both technique and text allows the reader to repeat the research procedure, giving it reliability. That is, the reader can use my procedure on the texts and compare his or her interpretations with mine. I am not arguing, of course, that this approach solves all problems of validity-reliability but only that it does deal with them as well as any other existing procedure.

To give a crude comparison: Most qualitative studies emphasize validity, direct perception of phenomena, but sacrifice reliability (repeatability) since they seldom describe their techniques explicitly and include verbatim texts. Similarly, quantitative studies emphasize reliability but sacrifice validity. Techniques are described explicitly, but the raw data are virtually never presented and are seldom available even on request. Like qualitative and quantitative studies, the present approach represents a compromise between the conflicting demands of reliability and validity.

The basic innovation in my approach is that it allows for an analysis of complex events that integrates relevant viewpoints and includes diverse kinds of data at many levels; this approach is both interdisciplinary and multilevel. As will be suggested in the chapters that follow, many of the most significant components of protracted conflict seem to be just outside the field of vision of most disciplines and methods; because of disciplinary boundaries and procedural constraints, they are inadvertently excluded from consideration. As already suggested, my approach also imposes some arbitrary limitations. In the chapters that follow, both strengths and limitations will become apparent.

References

Gaylin, W. 1984. *The Rage Within.* New York: Simon and Schuster.

Goffman, E. 1967. *Interaction Ritual.* Garden City, NY: Anchor Books.

Gottschalk, L., C. Wingert, and G. Gleser, 1969. *Manual of Instruction for Using the Gottschalk-Gleser Content Analysis Scales.* Berkeley and Los Angeles: Univ. of California Press.

Lewis, H. 1971. *Shame and Guilt in Neurosis.* New York: International Universities Press.

Peirce, C. S. [1908] 1955. "Abduction and Induction." In *Philosophical Writings of Peirce.* New York: Dover.

Retzinger, S. 1991. *Violent Emotions: Shame and Rage in Marital Quarrels.* Newbury Park, CA: Sage.

Scheff, T. J. 1990. *Microsociology: Discourse, Emotion, and Social Structure.* Chicago: Univ. of Chicago Press.

Scheff, T. J., and S. M. Retzinger. 1991. *Emotions and Violence: Shame and Rage in Destructive Conflicts.* Lexington, MA: Lexington Books.

Simmel, G. 1955. *Conflict and the Web of Group-Affiliations.* Glencoe, NY: Free Press.

1

Quarrel and Impasse in a Marriage

The public and private worlds are inseparably connected. ... The tyrannies and servilities of one are the tyrannies and servilities of the other.

—**Virginia Woolf, *Death of the Moth***

The subject of this book, the causes of war, is vast and complex enough to be intimidating. So as not to intimidate the reader, this chapter concerns conflicts on a much smaller scale, at the level of relationships in a family. To help the reader grasp my argument, most of this chapter is devoted to a brief passage from the recording of an actual marital dispute and to my explanation of its causes.

Understanding, or at least holding an image in mind, of this particular marital dispute will be preparation for the subsequent chapters, which concern large-scale conflict. My explanation of the causes of war requires close understanding of three ideas: protracted conflict, alienation, and feeling traps. The strategy of this chapter is to show the reader how these ideas look when applied on a very small scale—to a quarrel between two people.

Protracted Conflict

This marital dispute oscillates between two types of conflict: interminable quarrels and silent impasses. If you have ever had a prolonged dispute with a parent or, if you are a parent, with your child, or with your spouse, you may already know what such quarrels and impasses are like. One thing you may already know about an interminable quarrel is that when it occurs, there are few surprises. You know that if you bring up a certain issue, a quarrel will ensue. Since you have had this same quarrel many times before, you know what you will say, how the other person will respond, how you will then respond, and so on. The quarrel seems to have a life of its own.

You may also be familiar with the silent impasse. Seeking to avoid a quarrel, both sides evade the issue. Quarrels and impasses seem to be opposite ways of dealing with conflict. As I use the term, quarrels have two characteristics: A topic of disagreement is discussed explicitly, and with this discussion, anger is shown by one or both combatants. The defining characteristics of impasses are the exact opposite: The topic of disagreement is avoided, and there is no show of anger. In the marital dispute discussed here, quarrel and impasse are two sides of the same coin, a protracted conflict.

Because I include impasse as a phase of protracted conflict, my discussion is considerably broader than the literature on group conflict. Thorson (Kriesberg et al., 1989, p. 3) defined a similar concept, "intractable conflict," as a dispute that stubbornly resists resolution. However, it is clear in his discussion and in those of others in the literature on this topic that this view is limited to the quarrel phase. By focusing only on wars, this view omits the peaceful processes that lead to wars. I illustrate this idea first on a small scale, an episode in a family conflict.

Although unending family conflict may develop on any subject, some common topics in a marriage are household chores or fittings and decor, children, money, sex, and faithfulness or love. Between parents and young children, common quarrel topics are homework, grades and motivation, and household tasks. Between parents and older children, familiar topics of conflict are clothing, appearance, money, education, careers, and choice of associates, especially dates. Examples are the character of the child's boy- or girlfriend, or too much makeup on a daughter's face.

Whatever the topic, we already know that a quarrel on a certain subject will end in bad feelings on both sides and that absolutely no headway will be made toward solving the problem. This knowledge is the main reason for silent impasses; we attempt to avoid open conflict. The puzzling thing about these quarrels is that, although we know they are futile and hurtful, at times we find it almost impossible to resist being drawn into them once the issue is raised. Sometimes we find ourselves raising the issue even though we had intended to avoid the matter entirely. At other times the other person brings it up. Who starts the quarrel does not seem to matter, however; it always follows its fated course.

If you cannot remember being involved in such quarrels or impasses, reading this chapter several times may help jar your memory. The rest of this book will be much easier to follow if you understand the dispute between Rosie and James not only from the outside, objectively, but also from the inside, as something that applies to you as much as to them. The basic message of this book is that war is not just *out there*, separate from us; it is also *in here*, inside of us.

From what has been said so far, it is easy to see the elements that all protracted conflicts share: They are repetitive, hurtful, futile, and compulsive, that is to say, involuntary. With regard to the disputed issue, both sides seem to be out of control. I do not mean out of control in the sense of screaming or hitting since these conflicts need not involve such antics. Indeed, protracted conflict occurs in some families in which there are never any quarrels, only impasses. The relationship between Rosie and James is almost entirely impassed. There are, however, families in which conflict involves screaming or, in some cases, physical violence. But in most families, this does not occur.

The typical family may call its quarrels "arguments" or "squabbles." These episodes need not be loud or long to have the features noted (repetitiveness, hurtfulness, futility, and compulsiveness). Although they are sometimes lengthy, they may also be quite brief, a few minutes or less. (The quarrel to be described lasted less than a minute.) Even brief quarrels of this type leave a residue of resentful or hurt feelings, which subside only very slowly.

A crucial feature of protracted conflict is the intimate relationship between its two poles: quarrels and impasses. When the quarrel is over, both sides withdraw, licking their wounds. Sometimes, but not always, one or both combatants may feel guilt or remorse about the wounds that they may have caused in the other person. The important point, however, is that since the quarrel is not resolved, the time between quarrels is not a real peace, only a temporary cessation of hostilities. One or both parties may act as if the dispute never happened or at least as if it will never happen again. They may not only act in this way but also believe it. Yet the attitudes and feelings on both sides that gave rise to the quarrel have not changed. Between quarrels both parties lie low, in wait for the next round. Conflicts are protracted if they occur at all times; then war and peace are only phases of a single continuing episode of alienation between the parties.

Silent impasses are the periods between quarrels. Although no anger is shown there is usually considerable tension "in the air" around the topic of dispute. Both parties seek to avoid the disputed topic, but they feel as if they are walking on eggshells. They may also harbor feelings of resentment or guilt as a result of the last quarrel and, underlying that, all the quarrels that preceded the last one.

For reasons that will become apparent in subsequent chapters, the existence of even a single impassed topic in a relationship has a tendency to spread to other topics, eventually coloring the whole relationship. The more conflict is evaded on each impassed topic, and the more such topics there are in a relationship, the less trust and affection appear. And the less chance there is of resolution since it is difficult to reach a mutually agreeable solution in silence. Just as relationships marked by interminable quarrels are too hot to handle, those marked by silent impasses are too cold. As the evasive tactics and the number of impassed topics increase, the temperature in a relationship may approach the emotional equivalent of absolute zero.

The amount of awareness that combatants have of their conflict varies. In some relationships both parties are aware to the point that their fighting (or impasse) is actually discussed (which may or may not itself end in a quarrel). Oddly enough, awareness does not necessarily decrease the amount of conflict, although in some cases it proves to be the first step toward a more peaceful relationship. Since unending conflict is compulsive, talking politely about it may also lead nowhere.

At the other extreme of awareness, some combatants seem oblivious to their conflict, acting as if, and even believing that, they have an ideal relationship. Typically, however, combatants have a partisan awareness, seeing the other person as blameworthy and themselves as innocent. Participants may notice that their conflict is futile but see it as entirely the fault of the other person. They note the other's repetitiveness, hurtfulness, and compulsion but manage not to be aware that they also behave in this manner. Because of the denial of self-responsibility, and the blaming of the other for everything, unending quarrels or impasses (or a combination of the two) build up a wall of self-righteousness on both sides. The more each person blames or ignores the other, the more self-righteous and defensive each becomes.

Understanding protracted conflict requires explaining its compulsiveness. When we know that a dispute is irrational, that it will be repetitive, hurtful, and futile, why do we continue it? Just as important as understanding the compulsion to fight is finding ways that participants or onlookers can stop fighting. The chapters in this book address both these questions in general terms.

Rather than beginning with a general explanation, I want to investigate a particular conflict, an actual marital quarrel taken from a larger study.[1] By looking closely at *what* was said by husband and wife and at *how* it was said moment by moment, Retzinger showed the specific causes of this brief conflict and what might have been done to either avoid it or resolve it once started. I am betting that understanding this tiny battle will help the reader follow my explanation of a vast and protracted war.

Following Retzinger, my approach to endless conflict between Rosie and James points toward two interrelated causes. The first concerns respect and emotion: Both husband and wife show lack of respect toward each other, and both hide their own emotions and ignore the emotions of the other. However, disrespectful behavior and hiding of emotions need not lead to unending conflict. The second cause concerns the participants' awareness. Disrespect and hidden emotions lead to the quarrel/impasse pattern only if both parties are unaware of their own behavior and feelings.

If both persons' disrespect and emotions are thoroughly disguised, then the stage is set for endless conflict. The dispute becomes a labyrinth, with layers and layers of thoughts, feelings, and behaviors so concealed that the conflict seems inevitable and insoluble. In the excerpt examined here, thoughts and feelings are hidden behind a veil of politeness and reasonableness.

In the last twenty years, Retzinger and I and other social scientists with a linguistic bent have been developing techniques subtle enough to penetrate the veil

---

1. This case is one of the four described in Retzinger (1991).

of disguises in interpersonal and intergroup communication. Perhaps the principal tool in this direction has been understanding the minute details of dialogue. In the excerpt that follows, many of the rabbit punches are so subtle that they can be seen only in slow motion and stills. To slow down the action, I analyze this excerpt word by word and gesture by gesture.

An Empirical Approach to Alienation

As indicated, the case I am using for illustrative purposes is from a larger study of marital conflict by Retzinger (1991). My discussion of the feeling trap concept and my analysis of the feeling trap in this particular dispute are based on her earlier work and that of Lewis (1971), who first discovered the pattern of shame alternating with anger. However, Tomkins (1963) had written earlier of shame-anger "binds," which may be a similar idea. I elaborate on the concept of feeling traps here and illustrate it in the case.

My analysis of social integration (alienation and solidarity), however, goes beyond the Retzinger study. She discussed the relation of alienation to conflict abstractly, noting Simmel's dictum that conflict is caused by separation rather than the other way around. Like Simmel and other social theorists, however, Retzinger did not apply this idea to word-by-word social interaction. Here I develop a linguistic method for determining the degree of integration between persons at every moment of contact.

The concept of social integration, of the balance between solidarity and alienation, is basic to sociological theory. It was particularly prominent in Marx's social theory, where it was an explicit core for his analysis. It was also central to Durkheim's basic study *Suicide* ([1897] 1952) and prominent in virtually all his work. Although he did not use the term *alienation*, it was clearly implied in his study of suicide.

Durkheim ([1897] 1952) sought to explain the constancy of suicide rates in religious and other groups in terms of the types of social relationships in each group. He showed, for example, that rates of suicide in predominantly Catholic regions in Europe were consistently and uniformly lower than rates in predominantly Protestant regions. He also considered variations in rates between nations and between occupations. These observations led him to formulate a cultural theory of suicide: Differences in culture lead to variations in suicide rates because culture influences the types of social relationships that prevail in a group.

At the core of Durkheim's theory of suicide is the distinction that he made between two kinds of cultures. On the one hand, there are cultures that are suicidogenic because they give too much prominence to individuals (as against the group), a characteristic of modern industrial societies. In his formulation, such cultures lead to egoistic or anomic suicide. On the other hand, there are cultures that give too much prominence to the group, such as the cultures of small traditional societies, which leads to what he called "altruistic" or "fatalistic suicide."

Durkheim sought to explain high suicide rates in traditional groups (too little emphasis on individuals), which led to culturally prescribed forms of suicide (as in hara-kiri in Japan), and in groups promoting change and innovations (too much emphasis on the individual), such as the most ascetic forms of Protestantism. Although Durkheim did not use the terms *solidarity* and *alienation,* his analysis was clearly focused on what would today be called "social integration," the issue of being either too loosely or too tightly bound to the group.

In his analysis, Durkheim took two important steps: He formulated an abstract theory of suicide, and he gathered data that supported his theory. In combining these two steps into a single study, he invented modern sociology. It seems to me, however, that a sociology composed of these two steps is not the last word. Durkheim's explanations of the link between his abstract concepts and his data were phrased in quite vague terms. A careful description of the process that links abstract concepts to empirical data seems to be necessary for the formulation of a complete theory.

Explicit models that link concepts (names for precisely defined abstract classes) to actual data are characteristic of successful sciences. The periodic table, which classifies the chemical elements, is an example: its form is finished because it grows organically out of a micromodel of the atom. In contrast, Linnaean classification in biology is a continuing embarrassment because it is still an arbitrary taxonomy: There is no underlying micromodel of the processes that lead to speciation to give form to the classification.

Durkheim's classification of the types of suicide is Linnaean since he did not specify a precise model of the process through which types of social relationships at the microlevel lead to suicide rates at the macrolevel. His theory gives a bird's-eye view of society, but suicide rates are discrete events. How can the two levels be connected?

I propose that micro- and macrolevels can be linked through specification of precise models of causation at the level of individuals, as I do in this book. In this way, I seek to give a systematic basis for what Giddens (1984) called "instantiation" and Geertz (1983) named "thick description" of a single case.

I am not arguing, however, that micro theories such as Durkheim's are unnecessary. I propose that theory construction at each level is equally necessary. By moving back and forth rapidly from the top down and from the top up, we may be able to advance understanding much more quickly than isolated efforts in each direction do. I describe a bottom-up strategy as one step toward building a theory of conflict.

In this book, I show how language use can be an indicator of the state of the social bond between two people. I focus on the use of pronouns, particularly I, you, we, and it. The disposition of these pronouns within a sentence and the relative weight accorded them can be used as cues to three different states of the bond: solidarity, isolation, and engulfment.

My approach partially overlaps with Buber's (1958) discussion of I-thou. What I call "solidarity language" (I-I) corresponds exactly to his I-thou. What I call the "language of isolation" (I-you) corresponds exactly to his I-it. I use different terms because Buber, like most philosophers and social scientists, did not consider the other form of alienation, what Bowen (1978) called "engulfment" (me-I). The idea of engulfment (sometimes called emeshment or fusion) is centrally important in family systems theory but is absent elsewhere in the human sciences. Social scientists usually confound engulfment with solidarity.

My use of I and me is quite different from Mead's (1934). His social psychology seemed to assume perfect solidarity, without any attention to the possibility of alienation. In Mead's scheme, the me is made up of the internalized representation of the roles of others. For example, the citizen utilizing a criminal court is prepared by already knowing the role of the judge, the jury, the police officer, the jailor, etc.

Mead never considered the degree to which each member of a society accurately know the roles of the other members. By ignoring this issue, he evaded the issue of imperfect relationships, of alienation. One example will suggest some of the difficulties with his approach. Consider the doctor-patient relationship. It is immediately obvious that the patient has only a superficial knowledge of the doctor's role and that the superficiality of that knowledge can cause impediments to cooperation. For instance, since the patient understands very little of what the doctor knows of the relationship between the patient's illness and the medication that the doctor has prescribed for treatment, the patient might fail to follow the doctor's orders. The relationship is asymmetric in this way.

The relationship is also asymmetric in another, more surprising way. Although the patient has never learned the role of the doctor, the doctor should certainly know the role of the patient, having been one before becoming a doctor and continuing to be one as a doctor. We would expect, therefore, that the doctor would understand patients. But as it turns out, such is not necessarily the case. As part of their medical training and as part of the management of roles, many doctors seem to "forget" the patient's experience; they do not understand their patients, not because of a lack of knowledge, but because of the emotional barriers that doctors erect against patients.

This process of forgetting also occurs in the teacher's role. Most teachers call very little upon their own role as students to guide their teaching; rather, their teaching seems to conform to the way other teachers teach. Once teachers have learned a body of knowledge, they seem to repress the difficulties they had in learning it, which erects a wall between them and their students. In the language I use here, teachers are engulfed with other teachers and isolated from students. Bimodal alienation, as I call it, seems to be the most common form of social relationship in the modern world.

A theoretical approach to alienation that is similar to my own is found Elias's (1987) discussion of the "I-self" (isolation) and the "we-self" (engulfment). Elias discussed the "I-we balance" (solidarity) in a way that is quite similar to my usage, except that he did not apply it to actual instances. These ideas can now be applied to an actual dialogue.

A Flare-up Between Rosie and James

The couples in Retzinger's study volunteered to have one of their arguments videotaped. The research followed a standard format (Gottman, 1979), which divides a forty-five minute taping into three equal segments: (1) neutral (each partner recounted events of her or his day); (2) conflict (partners discussed a "topic of frequent argument"); and (3) positive (partners discussed activities they enjoyed doing together). The original researcher, who used this format with a very large number of couples, reported that it never once failed to elicit a real quarrel, which was also Retzinger's experience.

The husband and wife in this case are both white and middle class, ages thirty-five and thirty-two, and married for eleven years. James, employed in the forestry service, had completed four years of college. Rosie was a college undergraduate at the time of the study. They were in a trial separation, living in separate towns: Rosie near her school, James close to his job. They had been discussing divorce.

The topic of their argument concerned one of their many disagreements: James's ownership of a private airplane, his "pride and joy," as he put it. Rosie had the opposite attitude, saying she "hated" the plane. Both husband and wife had told the author that, although the issue of owning the airplane was a very sore point between them, they had never actually argued about it. Instead, they agreed, Rosie would sometime express irritation very briefly but then back down. This is what happened in the following excerpt. Both partners had indicated to the interviewer that over the previous several years they had become increasingly tense and less affectionate with each other, which is characteristic of impassed relationships.

1.	23.25	**R:** so what aspects of the plane do you want to talk	
2.		about?	
3.		**J:** oh just airplanes in general it doesn't have to	impasse
4.		be	
5.		**R:** oh	
6.		**J:** specifically the one we have now (laugh)	
7.	30.09	**R:** no I wanna NARROW it RIGHT down TO that one	
8.		**J:** because I don't plan on it being the last the	
9.		end of the line	

10.		**R:** NO well I don't either not for you	quarrel
11.		**J:** oh good	
12.		**R:** no I wouldn't take your toy from you	
13.		**J:** all right	
14.		**R:** I I sacrificed a LOT for you to have toys (1.79)	
15.		(both laugh tightly)	

16.	49:00	**R:** but you didn't ask for it and I resent later and	impasse
17.		we're still going over it ok	
18.		**J:** Yeah it (3) it uh goes back to another era	

The main focus of this transcription is the words that were spoken, with only a few indications of nonverbal elements (the capitalized words indicate loud speech; the separation of some of the lines, interruptions). In a very detailed analysis of this argument, Retzinger (1991) also included second-by-second descriptions of many other nonverbal components that she observed in the videotape, including facial expression and changes in posture and gaze direction. My analysis of words and gestures is a condensed paraphrase of her much more detailed one.

Lines 7–15 can be seen as an extremely brief quarrel representing a disruption of the couple's normal mode of conflict, the silent impasse. As already indicated, Rosie and James's approach to their disagreement about owning the plane, as with all their other disagreements, has been to avoid talking about it. Because of this approach, no resolution of their various disagreements is occurring. Instead, they are considering divorce.

At the researcher's request, they try to confront their conflict over the plane. However, the actual confrontation is brief, only nine lines (about nineteen seconds). After line 15, the mood shifts from quarrel, with clear indications of conflict (loud talk, rapid speech, and mutual interruption), to polite discussion of the advantage and disadvantages of owning a plane (and many other topics treated in a similar way). Although several additional flare-ups can be found in the transcript of this dispute, they are even briefer than the one to be discussed here and much less intense. These later episodes of "bristle" are so short and low-keyed that Rosie and James both seem largely unaware of them. Rather than talk about the problem they are having in their relationship, they talk about a series of topics.[2] By becoming "rational," which in this case means abstract and theoretical, rather than concrete and personal, they avoid having to confront each other's desires and feelings.

---

2. The distinction between topic talk and relationship talk is an important part of the family systems approach (Watzlawick et al., 1967).

Here is an example of James in the rational mode (part of a turn than began in the fifty-fifth second): "I like ... the ability to just go down and jump in [the plane]. ... There's pro's and con's of course. There's times when the plane is broken; ... it'd be nice ... if ... you could just tell [the rental agency] you want another one." After the quarrel in lines 7–15, for virtually the rest of the time available for discussing the disagreement, James and Rosie remained in this "rational," objective mode.

If their habitual mode of handling conflict was evasion, how did they even manage a brief quarrel? A close look at the interaction suggests that they had a misunderstanding and that it was this misunderstanding that led to the brief confrontation. If we look closely enough at the words and gestures, we can understand not only the cause of this quarrel but also the key elements in their relationship as a whole. A detailed examination of the actual verbal and nonverbal components of this dispute suggests that it is a microcosm, representative of key aspects of their entire relationship.

Rosie opens their argument by asking a question in an ingratiating, childlike manner: "So what aspect of the plane do you want to talk about?" (lines 1 and 2). Since both Rosie and James know that it is Rosie who has a problem with the plane (she was the one who suggested that it be the topic of their argument), James misinterprets her question. Rosie might have begun by being direct about her desires and feelings about the plane: *"James, you know I have strong feelings about your plane."[3] After her introductory sentence, which would likely get an affirmative response from him indicating that he was ready to hear about her feelings, she could have stated them forcefully: *"I hate the plane and wish we would get rid of it!" In actuality, she does not make a strong statement but instead asks a question in a submissive way. James appears to interpret this message to mean that she may continue to avoid confrontation and he can do likewise.

His error is soon clear, however, since Rosie interrupts his answer ("airplanes in general") with an "Oh" indicating surprise (line 5). When James continues to finish his sentence (line 6), Rosie quickly and openly contradicts his answer with a "No" (line 7) followed by a strong statement that she wishes to do the exact opposite of what he wants. She does want to talk, not about planes in general, but about the particular one they own (line 7).

There are many indications of anger in Rosie's response to James's statement. Her interruption in line 5, her very quick response to line 6, and the rapidity of her speech are one set of indications. The flat contradiction in her "No," her wish for the opposite of his suggestion, the loud intonation given to some of the words, an aggressive leaning forward as in a challenge, the narrowing of her eyes, and the lowering of her eyebrows (as reported by Retzinger) all suggest anger.

---

3. As is conventional in linguistics, the asterisk * indicates a hypothetical, a statement that could have been made but was not.

Rosie's anger at this point may indicate an important trait. That she gets angry at James for avoiding confrontation when she has just done the same suggests that she may be quite unaware of the part she herself plays in creating their conflict. This clue is especially strong because the plane is very much her issue.

James's response to Rosie's angry contradiction suggests that he also becomes angry. His anger, however, is expressed less by his nonverbal gestures than by his words. Rosie's face, posture, and intonations dramatically express anger. Aside from some fluster (interrupting himself to change the end of the sentence), laughter at some of his words, and his fixed smile becoming slightly more tense, there is much less change in James's manner than in Rosie's. But his words indicate a rapid shift from conciliation to attack: "because I don't plan on it being … the end of the line." The implication is that what Rosie wants does not matter to him, a very abrupt and rejecting declaration. Rosie reacts to this line as if it is extremely hurtful to her; she becomes sarcastic as well as intensely angry.

Rosie's next three turns express anger and sarcasm. She continues to lean forward with an expression of anger on her face. The beginning of line 10 starts with agreement, that the present plane will not be the last one. But by the end of the line, Rosie gives it a nonverbal twist that suggests separation from James. She drags out the last word "you" into two syllables, "you-ou," with the last syllable being the longest, her face expressing contempt and, more faintly, disgust. Her message suggests that she has had all of James that she can bear, that he is a hopeless case. It clearly indicates that she sees him as different, separate from herself.

In line 12, she continues the attack. Both her words and manner continue to indicate hostility. In this line, there is a new note, however, of condescension and contempt. She calls his airplane a toy. Beginning at this point, she is no longer offering him respect for an equal, another full adult like herself; she treats him as a childish adult.

In line 14, she again calls his plane a toy, once again implying that he is acting like a child. Line 14 contains another word spoken loudly, suggesting not only that "she sacrificed a LOT for James to have toys" but also that she is angry about having made the sacrifice.

After line 14, the mood of Rosie's responses abruptly changes. Line 16 contains one word indicative of anger ("resent"), but it is now encased between conciliatory words and ideas: James did not ask her for the sacrifice, and they are discussing it. Moreover, the manner of Rosie's delivery also changes from the sharp, loud staccato of lines 7–14 to an oversoft musing, almost as if addressed to herself rather than to James. To understand this sudden shift, let us look at James's response to Rosie's angry outbursts in lines 7–14.

Before Rosie's first angry line (7), James had spoken in full sentence form. After line 7, the length of his responses decreases considerably: His two subsequent responses are all quite brief; each is only two words long. These two words suggest agreement with Rosie, but his manner contradicts his words. In all three responses, he seems to be withdrawing from the conversation. His line 11 is delivered much more quietly than his earlier responses. Lines 13 and 18 continue to be soft. By line 13, his fixed smile has begun to fade, and there are subtle signs that he is shrinking down into his seat. By line 18, his fixed smile has returned, after Rosie has begun to make amends, but he is stammering and still mumbling.

After line 14, it appears that Rosie has noticed the indications of James's withdrawal. As she explained to the interviewer, there is a brief bristle of anger; then one or the other backs down. Perhaps Rosie felt that her angry outbursts had hurt James's feelings or that he might break off the discussion if she persisted. At any rate, it is clear that by line 16, Rosie has swallowed her anger, changing to a much more distanced kind of rational discussion. After a brief confrontation, she has backed down. The couple has returned to the status quo, an impasse in which the issues that separate them are avoided.

Feeling Traps

Rosie and James actually disagree about the ownership of the plane. What issue is their rational discussion of ownership and renting avoiding? Late in their discussion, Rosie hints at this issue; she suggests that the plane might be just a convenient target for her anger. But at this point she is stymied. She knows she has strong feelings, but she also feels that James is entitled to his plane. She does not know how to deal with her feelings or how to articulate their sources.

By piecing together various parts of Rosie's comments, Retzinger inferred the feelings that are being displaced onto the plane. Rosie seems to feel that James is more interested in the plane than in her. Perhaps she feels that he is using the plane as a way of avoiding her. She feels unheard and rejected.

James also seems to feel rejected, but for different reasons. It appears that he sometimes wants to avoid Rosie because she seems irritable and critical of him. Although he never uses the word *nag*, his imagery suggests it. Both he and Rosie feel neglected and unloved. If this inference is correct, it would go far in explaining a puzzling aspect of the relationship: the intensity of their anger, resentment, and disaffection.

Both Rosie's anger and James's anger seem excessive in terms of the reasons that have been given so far for this feeling. At the beginning of the quarrel, Rosie reacts with an intense display of anger and flat contradiction to James because his statement is not what she wants. James reacts to her anger with an abrupt and bitter statement excluding her from consideration. In addition to these stimuli to anger, something else is probably also occurring that adds fuel to the flame.

Retzinger's analysis suggested that Rosie and James are unintentionally humiliating each other and that it is humiliation that powerfully amplifies their anger and other emotions. Rosie seems to have already been in a state of shame in line 1, as indicated by the licking of her lips, false smile, tentativeness, and passive questioning mode. She may hear James's attempt to help her further evade confrontation differently from what he intends. She may think that if he really loves her, he will introduce her issue for her. Since he does not, she may feel rejected, a state of seeming unworthy to the other (shame).

When Rosie responds angrily, James, too, may well feel unloved. *"She gets angry at me for nothing: for trying to help her out of a jam." The slight changes in his manner that take place during Rosie's line 7—laughing words, fluster, and tense smiling—are all indicative of a shame state, as is his verbal and nonverbal withdrawal. In this initial exchange, both Rosie's anger and James's seem to have been preceded by a type of shame that is visible to the observer of the videotape but invisible to the participants.

Their lack of awareness of their own emotions was borne out in the debriefing session that Retzinger held several weeks after the taping. After viewing the entire tape, the subjects asked to see some of the episodes again. Retzinger paused the tape at moments of high emotion without making any comment. Both Rosie and James reacted with surprise to their own appearance.

When the tape was paused the first time at the peak of Rosie's anger in the passage described here, Rosie pointed to her own image on the screen, saying, "*That* is one angry woman." She explained to Retzinger that at the time she was unaware that she was angry. She reacted in a similar way to other passages, as did James. When the tape was stopped toward the end of the passage described here, James turned to Rosie, saying, "*That's* the expression on my face that you have been telling me about." He was referring to his tense, withdrawing, shrinking look, which he called his "hurt" look. Apparently they were unaware of their own emotional expressions at the time of the quarrel.

Viewing their facial expressions as still images when the videotape was paused, Rosie and James could recognize Rosie's anger but not her moments of shame and embarrassment. Neither Rosie nor James could recognize James's anger, but both saw what they called "hurt" in his face. (As will be discussed later, "hurt" turns out to be a codeword for feelings of rejection, that is to say, shame.) Although they were originally unaware of their own emotions, viewings of the videotape led them to recognize some, but not all, of the emotions relevant to their unending conflict.

It is relevant to this discussion that Rosie and James reacted very strongly to what they saw in the tape. (In contrast, many of the other couples participated perfunctorily in the debriefing session; in some cases, one or both of the subjects did not attend at all.) Rosie and James extended the session (three hours rather than the usual one hour) and benefited from it. In a follow-up three years later, they were living together again. Rosie told the interviewer that the debriefing session had changed their lives. She also said that, although James still had his plane, it no longer stood between them. Participation in the study had led them in directions that had changed their relationship for the better.

Hidden Shame

To introduce the idea of a feeling trap, let me retrace the cues to emotion shown by Rosie and James in the dialogue under discussion, this time in sequence. Both Rosie and James seem to be embarrassed (which I take to mean a mild shame) during the first part of this segment (lines 1–6, designated as an impasse). Both show false smiles, and both are soft-spoken and evasive about the topic to be discussed. These are cues to shame.

During the quarrel stage (lines 7–15) Rosie bristles: She shows intense anger with her words and posture, facial expression, and gestures for a period of about nineteen seconds. James also shows anger during this period, but less dramatically than Rosie and for a much briefer period. In lines 8 and 9 (about two seconds), his words, although only slightly louder than his earlier comments, are abruptly rejecting of Rosie. For the rest of the quarrel stage, although Rosie is still showing anger, James shows many verbal and nonverbal shame cues.

Finally, in the second impasse period, at the end of the segment (lines 16–18) both Rosie and James produce shame cues. The change in mood for Rosie is abrupt: From her loud, stacatto, and brusque mode during the quarrel stage, she suddenly becomes soft-spoken and mumbling, with part of her line jumbled. James's cues are less dramatic. Although he speaks somewhat more audibly in line 18, he is still soft-spoken. There is also a clear combination of shame cues in this line that appears for the first time in his discourse: He has a long pause (three seconds), repeats himself ("it, it"), and uses speech filler ("uh").

Both Rosie and James are first embarrassed, perhaps about bringing up a topic that will produce discord. Rosie then gets angry when James follows her lead in evading the topic they planned to discuss. Then James gets angry, perhaps because Rosie is angry and disrespectful. As she continues to show anger toward him, the shifts in his behavior indicate withdrawal and shame. He continues to show shame cues to the end of this segment. Rosie seems to have noticed his withdrawal, which perhaps produces remorse and shame in her for being angry at James.

This review of emotion cues suggests that Rosie and James both go through a similar sequence of emotions: shame-anger-shame. Although Rosie's anger state lasts longer than James's, the pattern of emotions is the same for both of them, an alternation between shame and anger. As the reader will recall, all the shame and anger states that occurred during this episode seem to have been outside of awareness.

I use the term feeling trap to refer to episodes that involve the pattern just described: shame-anger alternations that occur largely outside of awareness. We seem to get angry at someone who insults or rejects us as a way of *avoiding* the painful feeling of shame. In this case anger serves as a substitute or defense against feeling shame. However, as in Rosie's lines 16–17, we may then feel ashamed of being angry. Apparently the alternation between shame and anger, if it goes completely unacknowledged, can become a closed loop, a self-perpetuating emotional "upset" that refuses to subside.

The example of Rosie and James also suggests that the loop of shame-anger is not only internal but also external. Both Rosie and James are each caught in an internal loop of shame and anger, but they are also reacting to each other's insulting and rejecting words and manner. Like two hot coals placed close together, the heat of one further inflames the other. The shame-anger feeling trap is one of the two motors that propel protracted conflict.

To summarize the discussion so far: The recorded dispute between Rosie and James began with a brief quarrel but quickly changed to an impasse. This dispute appeared to faithfully mirror their relationship, which was impassed at the time of the study and appeared to be breaking up. However, largely as a result of their participation in the study, Rosie and James took steps that changed and renewed their relationship. How can we account for their original conflict and the changes that took place in it?

Already mentioned as causes of their conflict were disrespect, the hiding of emotions, and Rosie and James's lack of awareness of these factors. To understand how these components lead to protracted conflict, we must look at the idea of alienation.

Two Forms of Alienation

Isolation

Human contact and cooperation require connectedness. The sociological term for this connectedness is solidarity. Alienation occurs when two parties are disconnected from each other. Solidarity between humans involves more than the kind of rigid unity found, for example, in an insect society because of the complexity of human beings and their society. Given this complexity, effective cooperation requires both conformity, what might be called "me" responses, and nonconformity, or "I" responses.

To solve the host of novel problems that confront us, we must find a balance between the I and the me. Too much emphasis on the individual leads to isolation and open conflict; too much emphasis on the relationship leads to hyperconformity and impasse (because individuals are not contributing their own distinctive points of view, which are needed for solving problems).

Understanding Rosie and James's dispute hinging on realizing that alienation comes in two opposite forms: isolation (the participants are too divided, too much I) and engulfment (too unified, too much me).[4] The interminable quarrel phase of protracted conflict involves alienation in the isolated form; the silent impasse phase, engulfment. Rosie and James's alienation in its isolated form occurs during the quarrel phase of their conflict.

On several occasions in the dialogue under review, the issue of language that implies separation between Rosie and James is mentioned. A flagrant instance occurs in line 10, where Rosie makes clear that she is seeing James as separate from herself ("I don't either, not for you-ou"). She agrees that this will not be the last plane, at least for him. The agreement in this case is purely verbal; her difference from him is rendered in nonverbal terms (the heavy emphasis and stretching out of the last word) and in her facial expression, which suggests contempt and disgust.

Rosie's statement illustrates an important point: Agreement or disagreement may be expressed in an unemotional, dispassionate way. Separation or division in a relationship, however, is largely an emotional matter. During this quarrel, Rosie and James are not only in disagreement over the topic of their argument (the plane); they are also emotionally separated from each other in their relationship. During the quarrel, it is clear that Rosie and James do not feel *connected*, but divided.

The difference between feeling connected and feeling divided can be demonstrated by some of the verbal and nonverbal components in the excerpt. The way in which Rosie and James use the pronouns *I, you,* and *we* suggests two different forms of discourse: the language of separation and the language of unity. These forms of language indicate alienation: Separation language is the outer form of isolation; unity language, of engulfment.

Before the quarrel starts (or at least before James is aware that he is involved in a quarrel), he uses the word *we* (line 6: "[It doesn't have to be] specifically the one *we* have now"). This we expresses James's sense of unity with Rosie; he sees himself and Rosie as together, as a couple at this moment.

We does not occur again until line 17 ("and *we*'re still going over it ok"), when Rosie backs down from the quarrel. The intervening nine lines bristle with the kind of I's and you's that emphatically signal separation between Rosie and James.

Line 7   (R): *I* want to narrow it right down."
Line 8   (J): *I* don't plan on it being the last."
Line 10 (R): *I* don't either not for *you.*"
Line 12 (R): *I* wouldn't take your toys from *you.*"
Line 14 (R): *I* sacrificed a lot for *you.*"

Note that the I comes first in all these lines. The I coming before the you seems to

4. The idea of isolation and of engulfment is due to Bowen (1978), one of the originators of family systems theory.

signal the relative importance of the two persons, with the speaker placing self in the foreground and the other person in the background. Another way of putting it is that in these lines the speakers are seeing self mostly as subject, as an I, but they are reducing the other to an object, a me.

The symbolic division between Rosie and James is most clearly signaled in Rosie's angriest three lines (10, 12, and 14). These lines are like a war chant: all have the same form and nearly the same length, the I-you segment begins with I and ends with you, and each line states a difference between Rosie and James. All three lines have the same forceful implication: *"You and I are NOT a unit; we are two separate individuals." Rosie is not seeing herself and James as unified but as divided.

Line 16 also contains I and you, but the spell is broken ("but *you* didn't ask for it and *I* resent later"). The you comes before the I and does not express a difference between them. The I in this line is an I that resents, but without the emotional vehemence of her last four lines. Unlike the earlier I's, whose meaning was clearly expressed, this I is in a clause whose meaning is vague and delivery is somewhat jumbled: "I resent later" is said so softly that it is difficult to understand the clause at first.

James's we in line 6 is an expression of unity before the quarrel begins, and Rosie's we in line 17 announces the quarrel's end. In between these two limits, both Rosie and James use I-you, rather than we, language. I-you language can be a language of separation, as it is here. Separation is a form of alienation.

During the quarrel segment, Rosie and James are alienated from each other in the sense of being isolated. Their alienation is expressed not only in their words but also in their manner. Rosie's manner extravagantly expresses scorn and contempt, divisive emotions. James's manner also expresses division, but much more subtly than Rosie's. His tense smile, stammering, self-interruption, and shrinking down into his seat suggest withdrawal.

It is clear that during the quarrel, separation language predominates completely over unity language since there are ten I's and you's indicative of separation and no we's. The next question is, What is the separation-unity score during the silent impasse segments of the dialogue? It turns out that unity language is clearly dominant over separation language.

Engulfment

Rosie's turn that ends the quarrel (lines 16–17) provides an example of unity language: "But you didn't ask for it and I resent later and we're still going over it ok." Unlike the four preceding turns, the you comes before the I in this turn. In the first clause, Rosie is making James, rather than herself, the subject of her comment. She is also justifying his actions rather than her own, in dramatic contrast to her three earlier turns.

Because the next clause ("and I resent later") is mumbled and ungrammatical, its meaning is not clear. In the context, however, Rosie seems to be saying that because her resentment arose after they had already bought the plane, she was not opposed to the plane at first. The implication once again, as in the first clause, is that the quarrel is not James's fault. The third clause ("and we're still going over it") also seems to further excuse James's actions: Although she is resentful of the plane, she should be grateful that James is still willing to discuss the matter. The last segment, only one phrase ("ok"), is a call for agreement or unity coming after three clauses that are also calls for unity. After four turns of nothing but separation language, here is a entire turn of unity language.

In this turn, a dramatic shift has taken place in the identity of the subject. In the preceding four turns, the speaker was the subject. In this turn, Rosie is no longer the subject of her comments. In the first segment, she refers to James (you) but not to herself. Again in the third and fourth segments, Rosie does not refer to herself but to we (explicitly in the third segment, implicitly in the fourth).

At first glance, Rosie's use of I in the second segment seems to make her the subject. However, this segment is hemmed in between segments in which she is not the subject and is murmured as if to herself. The softened and jumbled delivery of the segment suggests that the speaker is suppressing self as subject in the interest of a message of unity.

James explaining the pros and cons of owning a plane is another example of the speaker suppressing self as subject. The excerpt begins with James referring to himself as subject ("I like the ability to just go down and jump in the plane"), but in the four lines that follow, he does not refer to himself again. Instead of I's, he uses it's and you's. The it's and you's refer to persons in general and objects, which is a way of being objective rather than talking about himself as subject, his feelings, and his desires.

In using unity language, both Rosie and James become me's (objects) to each other rather than I's (subjects). Instead of giving voice to their own desires and feelings, each suppresses them in a show of unity. This occurs verbally and nonverbally. In the verbal component of unity language, Rosie and James each turn their own I (subject) into a me (object) by emphasizing you's, we's, it's, and objects rather than I's. Unity language also deemphasizes self by nonverbal means. When the pronoun *I* is used, it is likely to be lost among a host of you's, we's, and it's; spoken softly; and/or obscured by being a part of a vague or ungrammatical sentence.

A close examination of the Rosie-James videotape shows that the suppression of self in an engulfed relationship goes much deeper than language. There are subtle verbal and nonverbal signs that Rosie is still angry and ashamed in lines 16–17, but she is now suppressing these feelings. She is using the language of unity and in the interest of unity is suppressing her feelings.

James also suppresses his feelings in a show of unity. The anger that he expressed verbally in lines 8–9, and the shame he expressed nonverbally (withdrawal) during the quarrel are suppressed after line 17, as shown in his "pros and cons" turn, in the interest of unity. Rosie and James relinquish integral parts of themselves—their emotions—in their show of unity.

The characteristic of engulfment that makes it a form of alienation is that the parties suppress important parts of themselves for the sake of unity. In the aforementioned lines James and Rosie suppress their feelings. But engulfment means that any of the various parts of self may be sacrificed to unity: thoughts, beliefs, perceptions, and values, not just feelings.

Engulfment leads to massive conformity since self is subjugated to the other person or to the group. Rosie's submissive, childlike passivity in her opening line is an example. A wife inviting a husband to represent her position, rather than speaking for herself, suggests that stereotyped male and female roles in our society are a manifestation of engulfment. In the stereotyped female role, a woman is socialized so that first as a daughter, and then as a wife, she is submissive, an empty vessel, to complement the stereotyped male role of father or husband, the dominating leader in the family.

James's inexpressive manner of presenting himself shows how the giving up of parts of self is related to the stereotyped male role. Even when he is angry in the beginning of the quarrel, his anger is expressed only verbally, with little show of emotions. What he calls "hurt," his shame over being belittled by Rosie, is expressed only by withdrawal; he never verbalizes it or any other feelings in the whole dispute. As befitting the stereotyped male role of the powerful leader of the family, James has given up his right to express hurt and other vulnerable feelings.

We are accustomed to thinking of isolation as a form of alienation; we recognize separation and division as disconnection between persons. But engulfment is a more subtle form of alienation because disconnection between persons arises from disconnection from self. The childlike passivity that Rosie shows in her opening lines occurs because for the moment she has relinquished her own viewpoint, desires, thoughts, and feelings in regard to the plane. She has abandoned her emotions and her intelligence in order to act submissively.

In responding to Rosie's opening question with a line about planes in general, James also abandons parts of himself: his desire to own a plane, the resentment he seems to feel about Rosie's opposition, and perhaps some guilt about his own opposition to her. Like Rosie, he hides his desires and feelings to show unity with her.

Effective cooperation between human beings involves the ability to deal rapidly with complex and novel problems as they arise. Because of the complexity and novelty of the problems we face, solidarity requires that we draw upon our *whole* selves, and connect with the whole selves of other participants. Alienation occurs if important parts of self are withheld (engulfment) or if participants are completely divided (isolation).

Relationships of solidarity, isolation, and engulfment between persons are represented in Figure 1.1. Solidarity involves connectedness between selves. In alienation, disconnection between selves occurs. In isolation, there is disconnection because of division between the parties; in engulfment, because of division within the parties.

I have already discussed the features of discourse that indicate isolation and engulfment. I indicated how I-me communication (the language of separation) occurred between Rosie and James during their quarrel and how me-I language (the language of unity) occured during silent impasse. How does the language of solidarity differ from separation and from unity languages? As the reader might guess, solidarity language shows balance between separation and unity.

To highlight the passivity of Rosie's opening line, I previously introduced hypothetical statements for her: *"James, you know I have strong feelings about your plane," and *"I hate the plane and wish we could get rid of it!" These two lines show a relationship among I's, you's and we's that is different from both separation language and unity language.

The first segment of the first line names the other person, and the second segment ("you know") begins with a you; the third segment begins with an I. There is a mixture of you's and I's in this sentence, two you's and one I. Unity language dominates, but only slightly. The first segment of the second sentence begins with an I, but the second segment begins with a we. In this line there is one I and one we, a balance between separation and unity. In this hypothetical example, Rosie is the subject, she states her desires and feelings, but she does so without putting James in the position of an object. Indeed, she implies that he, too, is a subject by including his participation as part of the we in both lines. These two sentences contain features indicating both separation and unity.

These sentences are not perfect examples of balance in the language of solidarity since unity is somewhat dominant in the first one. But they have much more balance between unity and separation than any of the actual utterances by Rosie and James. The speaker treats both self and other as an I. Solidarity is manifested in I-I language rather than the I-me language of isolation or the me-I language of engulfment.

This discussion suggests that if a person uses solidarity language, disputes need not lead to alienation. Disconnection can be avoided if the speaker uses a language that is direct in revealing her or his desires and feeling but at the same time shows respect for the other's desires and feelings. I refer to this kind of communication as "leveling."[5] This combination of directness and respect may seem easy enough to achieve in the abstract, but it often turns out to be difficult to manifest without considerable practice.

The language of separation may be direct in revealing the speaker's desires and feelings, but it is disrespectful of the other person since it places that person in a lower position than the speaker. In contrast, the language of unity is respectful,

---

5. The idea of leveling is due to Satir (1972), another of the founders of family systems theory.

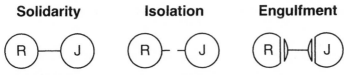

FIGURE 1.1 Three types of social relationships.

deferring to the view of the other person, but it suppresses the speaker's thoughts and feelings. Most of us have had little practice in leveling, in combining directness and respect, since we often equate directness with bluntness or rudeness and respect with complete deference to the other person.

The idea of leveling can be used to explain the change in Rosie and James's relationship that began to take place after the debriefing session. The most destructive features of their dispute tactics had been occurring outside of their awareness; neither Rosie nor James realized how disrespectful they were being or what emotions they were expressing. Apparently viewing themselves on videotape and discussing what they saw began to bring some of these tactics into awareness. Furthermore, during the debriefing session, they seemed to realize that they could level with each other about their desires and feelings without being disrespectful. For these reasons, changes began to take place in their communication style and in their expression of emotions, changes that established a stable basis for their marriage.

Rosie and James's original dispute style shows how dysfunctional communication styles, suppression of desires and feelings, and alienation are interrelated. The change in their relationship shows how leveling, expression of desires and feelings, and solidarity are interrelated. Leveling about their thoughts and feelings increased mutual understanding (solidarity), which led to the reestablishment of trust and affection.

The Motors of Protracted Conflict

The discussion so far points toward an explanation of the most puzzling feature of protracted conflict. How can it be that when we know a conflict is repetitive, hurtful, and futile we can be so irrational as to allow ourselves to continue it? The answer suggested earlier was that the parties to these conflicts are under compulsion to continue them, a compulsion they find difficult to resist. The discussion of alienation and feeling traps suggests a way of explaining this irrational compulsion.

There is now a considerable body of studies in the social and clinical sciences that suggests that basic communication tactics and styles of expressing emotions are learned very early in childhood. Dispute styles in families seem to be passed on from parents to children. Rosie and James's tactics may have been learned so early in childhood that they had disappeared from awareness long before the two met each other.

The repetitive tactics used in a particular family seem to survive, not because they are effective in solving disputes, but because they hide the pain of alienation and shame. People learn to distract thenmselves from feelings of frustration and humiliation by fighting about disagreements (quarrels) or by avoiding disagreements (impasses). After thousands of repetitions of these tactics, they become automatic, which is to say compulsive. Denial of painful feelings and emotions becomes a way of life.

The uncovering of hidden alienation and shame between Rosie and James could explain the compulsiveness of protracted conflict. The parties to the conflict experience constant alienation and shame, which may be the most painful of all feelings. Why do they act in ways that continue to generate these powerful feelings? There seem to be two motors in their relationship that are always running, the first being driven by unacknowledged shame, the second by alienation.

The feeling trap motor turns on when we get angry at someone who rejects or insults (shames) us and acts as a substitute for feeling the pain of rejection or insult. That is, being angry about being ashamed and ashamed about being angry can become a self-perpetuating loop of intensely painful feelings, usually much more painful than the original shame being defended against. A shame-anger loop of this type generates continuing resentment or, in more intense form, hatred. Since the shame that drives the shame-anger loop is outside of awareness (the anger may or may not be outside of awareness), the resulting aggression is compulsive.

Like feeling traps, alienation also can produce a self-perpetuating loop. Isolation between two parties is signaled by and leads to language that is disrespectul toward the other, which leads to further isolation. In engulfment, we suppress important parts of ourselves, either desires, thoughts, feelings, or some combination of these elements. Because we have not allowed our whole self to be expressed in an engulfed relationship, we are unable to solve problems at the core of the relationship, which leads to further alienation.

Shame-anger feeling traps and alienation do not exist independently of each other but feed into each other. Shame is crucially important in relationships in two distinct ways. First, shame serves as an automatic signal of moral trespass; we know when we have done wrong, regardless of the type of situation, when we feel ashamed. Second, shame helps us monitor the degree of unity and division in our relationships. This latter function connects feeling traps and alienation directly.

When there is too much unity, when someone comes too close to us, we feel exposed or invaded, which are both shame states. When there is too much division, when someone is too far from us, we feel invisible or rejected, which also are shame states. Shame cues enable us to regulate the distance between ourselves and others.

If shame signals are suppressed and/or ignored, we find it difficult to know where we stand with others, whether we are too far or too close. Under these conditions, relationships become stiff or rude; we find it difficult to get emotional satisfaction and to cooperate. Since shame-anger feeling traps and alienation are both caused by and produce the suppression of shame cues, each feeds into the other. The denial of shame and alienation are like different sides of the same coin. The denial of shame is the individual side of alienation, just as alienation is the social side of the denial of shame.

The shame-anger feeling trap and alienated communication tactics are motors that are always running; in tandem, they form a perpetual motion machine. It is this machine that gives rise to the cyle of insult and revenge that has left a bloody trail throughout human history. As will be discussed in Chapter 3, the insult-revenge cycle is visible in primitive warfare, duels, and feuds in most societies and eras of human history.

My explanation of the dispute between Rosie and James has shown that their dialogue contains the elements of this cycle. Both Rosie and James use only the language of alienation, both in its isolated and engulfed forms. Both display the cues for shame but are not aware of their own shame or the shame of the other person. During the impasse phases of the dialogue, both Rosie and James suppress their anger. During the quarrel phase, Rosie shows her anger in both verbal and nonverbal ways, but James shows his anger only verbally. Their conflict is protracted because they both use alienated language and are caught in a shame-anger feeling trap. The behavior of each person toward the other further intensifies the trap of each person.

Rosie and James could have continued this conflict forever. But in the debriefing session they began to learn leveling communication tactics and the acknowledging of their emotions. As a result of these changes, they avoided the divorce they had been planning.

Not all disputes lead to insult-revenge cycles; conflict can be contained through the efforts of the disputing parties, as in the relationship between Rosie and James after the debriefing session. Although avoiding insult in group competition is a more complex problem than in a marriage, many groups compete without generating protracted conflict. In competitive sports, for example, a good coach attempts to avoid alienating language and humiliation, not only of her or his own team, but also of the other team. For example, after the score is sufficiently high to indicate certain victory, the coach will substitute freely in an attempt to save face for the other team.

Conclusion

My analysis of the dispute between Rosie and James illustrates three principles concerning the causation and resolution of conflict:

1. Protracted conflict involves oscillation between periods of "peace" (silent impasses) and "war" (interminable quarrels).
2. Conflict of this type is caused by alienation between the combatatants, which takes two forms: unity (engulfment) during impasses and separation (isolation) during quarrels. A key aspect of alienation from self and others is the denial of shame, which results in a feeling trap within each party and one between them.
3. Protracted conflict can be resolved by the transformation of alienation into solidarity. Leveling communication generates understanding and trust, as does acknowledgment of shame. When shame is acknowledged, parties are able to regulate the distance between themselves so that at no time are they either too far or too close.

The rest of this book applies these principles to protracted conflict on a large scale. The book moves from an extremely small scale to an exceedingly large one. I propose that when leaders of nations and their followers face large-scale, emotionally charged conflicts, they utilize the only dispute tactics they know—the ones they learned, beneath the level of awareness, in their families.

Conventional wisdom holds that it is dangerous to assume that people in groups behave in the same way that individuals do. But it may be even more dangerous to assume that they do not. The issue is actually an empirical one that has been little investigated: Under what conditions and in what ways does group behavior repeat and differ from individual behavior? This book offers a preliminary attack on this problem.

Chapter 2 shows how denial of emotions, particularly the emotion of shame, arose in the history of our civilization. Chapter 3 outlines a general theory of individual and group conflict, utilizing the ideas of protracted conflict, shame-anger feeling traps, and alienation that were illustrated in the dialogue between Rosie and James. Chapters 4 and 5 apply these ideas to an understanding of the origins of the two world wars. Chapter 6 discusses current intergroup conflicts that were outcomes of issues left unresolved by the world wars and describes ways of resolving such intergroup conflicts.

References

Bowen, M. 1978. *Family Therapy in Clinical Practice*. New York: Jason Aronson.

Buber, M. 1958. *I and Thou*. New York: Scribner's.

Durkheim, E. [1897]. 1952. *Suicide*. London: Routledge.

Elias, N. 1987. *Involvement and Detachment*. Oxford: Basil Blackwell.

Geertz, C. 1983. *Local Knowledge*. New York: Basic Books.

Giddens, A. 1984. *The Constitution of Society*. Berkeley and Los Angeles: Univ. of California Press.

Glaser, B., and A. Strauss. 1963. *The Discovery of Grounded Theory.* Chicago: Aldine.

Goodwin, M. H. 1990. *He-Said-She-Said.* Bloomington: Univ. of Indiana Press.

Gottman, J. 1979. *Marital Interaction.* New York: Academic Press.

Kriesberg, L., T. A. Northrup, and S. J. Thorson, eds. 1989. *Intractable Conflicts and Their Transformation.* Syracuse, NY: Syracuse Univ. Press.

Lewis, H. B. 1971. *Shame and Guilt in Neurosis.* New York: International Universities Press.

Mead, G. H. 1934. *Mind, Self and Society.* Chicago: Univ. of Chicago Press.

Retzinger, S. 1991. *Violent Emotions: Shame and Rage in Marital Quarrels.* Newbury Park, CA: Sage.

Satir, V. 1972. *Peoplemaking.* Palo Alto, CA: Science and Behavior.

Scheff, T. J. 1986. "Toward Resolving the Controversy over 'Thick Description.'" *Current Anthropology* 27: 408–409.

_____. 1990. *Microsociology: Discourse, Emotion, and Social Structure.* Chicago: Univ. of Chicago Press.

Scheff, T. J., and S. M. Retzinger. 1991. *Emotions and Violence: Shame and Rage in Destructive Conflicts.* Lexington, MA: Lexington Books.

Tomkins, S. 1963. *Affect/Imagery/Consciousness.* New York: Springer.

Watzlawick, P., J. H. Beavin, and D. D. Jackson. 1967. *The Pragmatics of Human Communication.* New York: Norton.

Woolf, V. 1942. *Death of the Moth.* London: Hogarth.

PART ONE

Theory & Method

2
Pride and Shame: The Master Emotions

Suggesting that shame plays a significant role in producing conflict is a relatively new idea. Most discussions of the source of conflict concern material interests. Those discussions that do include emotions seldom mention shame; they focus instead on anxiety, fear, or anger. In fact, shame is hardly discussed in Western societies. If it is important, why is it so little noticed?

This chapter attempts to answer that question by reviewing what is known about shame and its obverse emotion, pride. It is clear that these two emotions occur in opposite situations: We feel pride with achievements, success, and acceptance and shame with errors, failures, and rejection. The opposing character of pride and shame can be seen with great clarity in small children. Children who succeed or are praised show obvious manifestations of pride: the smile of satisfaction with self, the direct gaze, and the increased expansiveness of the whole body, as suggested by the phrase "swelling with pride." The indications of shame in children are equally obvious: the lowered voice, the furtive gaze, and the hangdog or sheepish look.

Although we sometimes see clear signs of pride and shame in adults, these are much less frequent than in children. Does this mean that pride and shame are unusual emotions in adults or that they manifest differently? The latter seems the case: Pride and shame appear frequently in adults but in disguise. We put a good face on things to others and even to ourselves.

One indication of reticence surrounding pride and shame in Western societies can be found in the ways these words are used in ordinary conversations. (The situation in traditional societies, such as those in Asian countries, is somewhat different.) In Western societies, the word *shame* can be used in a casual way that does

---

Several parts of this chapter are based on Chapter 1 of Scheff and Retzinger (1991). Used with permission of the publisher.

not refer to a particular emotion: "What a shame!" could also be said as "What a pity!" The word is used much less frequently to refer seriously to a particular emotion. Shame is seen as a crisis emotion and a very intense one at that. "You should be ashamed of yourself" is an extremely strong criticism, and "I feel ashamed" is a powerful indication of painful feeling.

Language and Culture

The English language itself places restrictions on discussions of shame. All other European languages, in addition to the crisis emotion of shame (for example, in German, *Schande*), have an everyday shame (in German, *Scham*) that means shyness or modesty (Schneider, 1977). This everyday shame is always a positive attribute. In Spanish, for example, *vergüenza* has very much the same connotation as shame, the shame of disgrace, but *pudor* is a virtue, as are similar words in French and Italian. The nearest word to *pudor* in English is humility. Even though the word itself shows its original connection to shame (humiliation), in modern usage humility has lost its membership in the shame family. Lacking an everyday, positive dimension, the idea of shame has a dark, heavy, and threatening meaning in English.

Although the emotion of shame seems less dark and intense in French, German, or Spanish than in English, there is considerable evasiveness about it in all Western languages. Even the milder forms of shame, such as embarrassment, are likely to be evaded. For example, instead of simply saying, "I was embarrassed," most speakers are likely to use a circumlocution, such as "It was an awkward moment for me." Why would they say in a roundabout way what could be said directly?

To answer this question, we must investigate the origins of pride and shame, which will lead us into some fundamental aspects of the human condition. The origins of emotions such as fear, anger, and grief are widely recognized: Fear arises from danger to life and limb, anger from frustration, and grief from loss. Seeing the origins of pride and shame is not as straightforward. Shame seems to arise from our need to feel the right degree of *connectedness* with others. Shame is the emotion that occurs when we feel too close or too far from others. When too close, we feel exposed or violated; when too far, we feel invisible or rejected. Pride is the signal of being at the right distance: close enough to feel noticed but not so close as to feel threatened.

The need for the right degree of connectedness is so primitive that we take it for granted. The basic shame contexts—transgressing morally, making a mistake in public, being ridiculed or rejected—all involve the potential for exclusion or incorporation or the anticipation of exclusion or incorporation. The basic pride contexts—achievement or success, admiration or love—all involve notice and acceptance.

All societies train their members to balance closeness and distance, the interests of self and other. No society can long exist that vastly overreaches in one direction or the other. But different societies lean in different directions. Particularly pertinent for the present discussion, societies oriented more toward preserving traditional social forms than changing them lean toward being too close, what Bowen (1978) called "engulfment." In such societies, there is less focus on the individual than on the relationship and the group. These same ideas of closeness and distance were anticipated in Durkheim's ([1897] 1952) treatment of the cultures that have higher rates of suicide.

Societies that are more oriented toward change lean toward being too far, toward what Bowen called "isolation." In the world today, Western societies offer examples of relationships in which the mix of solidarity and alienation leans toward isolation. In Asian societies, the mix leans toward engulfed relationships. A mix that leans toward engulfment is associated with the overt style of shame; the mix that leans toward isolation is associated with the bypassed style. This is the reason that Western languages tend to evade mention of shame. Asian languages, tending toward the overt style of shame, feature prominent discussions of shame, even to the point of exaggeration.

The idea of connectedness between persons is slippery in Western societies. Our languages are hardly adequate for the job of describing it. The sociological term for connectedness is solidarity. Here I propose an intimate relationship between solidarity, pride, and cooperation, on the one hand, and alienation, shame, and conflict on the other. This chapter focuses on the emotional components of these relationships, pride and shame.

Although emotions have been a topic of serious discussion for thousands of years, they form one of the cloudiest regions of human thought. Any investigation of emotions is at hazard from its beginning since the concept itself is undefined. Even the most scholarly and scientific analyses depend on the use of vernacular terms such as anger, fear, grief, shame, joy, and love and the underlying presuppositions about emotion in our society. The field of emotions is less a body of knowledge than a jungle of unexamined assumptions, observations, and theories. Some of the roots of our contemporary attitudes toward emotion, and some of the puzzles we still share, can be seen in biblical and other historical sources.

Biblical Sources

The issue of shame arises very early in the Old Testament. Although the word is not used, it is implied in the story of Adam and Eve. When Adam tells God that he hid because he was naked, God asks, "Who told thee that thou wast naked?" God inferred that since Adam was ashamed of being naked, he had become self-conscious, that he had eaten of the forbidden fruit. In the biblical story, shame arises simultaneously with human self-consciousness. This event is portentous; it hints that shame may play a central role in the human drama.

The shame context of the story is shown in most portrayals of the expulsion from the Garden, with both Adam and Eve showing embarrassment or shame. In the painting by Massaccio, Eve shows her embarrassment by covering her breasts and loins, but Adam covers his eyes with both hands. Perhaps Adam is more profoundly ashamed than Eve since she covers only parts of her self. Adam, by covering his eyes so that he will not see or be seen, like a child does, may be trying to escape entirely from regarding God and from being regarded by him.

Adam and Eve are completely submissive to God's punishment: They are silent in the face of his harsh judgment. The very possibility of standing up to authority has not yet arisen. Their silence implies not only that God has condemned them but also that they have condemned themselves; their shame is complete.

The book of Genesis implies two crucial episodes in human development: the physical creation of humans by God and the shift from the paradisiacal life of human animals to that of self-conscious human beings. A third significant episode occurs in the book of Job. The protagonist does not suffer in silence under God's wrath, as Adam and Eve did. Rather, he confronts God with his misery, questioning the justice of his fate. The story of Job provides the first suggestion that hierarchy in the human social order is not inexorable, as it is in animal societies, but can be challenged. Job's confrontation with God is a stirring toward freedom from rigid compliance with the status quo just as the birth of self-consciousness created the potential for freedom from animal existence.

A historical equivalent can be found in Vico's ([1744] 1968) pronouncement, "The social world is the work of men" (rather than of God or nature). Unlike all other living creatures, humans have the potential for creating their own existence. Vico's statement was courageous; he was in danger of his life for challenging the absolute authority of the church and state.

Even today, escape from inexorable authority is still only partial. Most of us, most of the time, are emeshed in the status quo, the taken-for-granted social arrangements of our society, which seem to us absolute and unchangeable. Even though the status quo is only one particular version of many possible social orders, to those enmeshed in it, it seems eternal. To a large degree, human beings, like other animals but for different reasons, are cogs in a social machine. "Not for me the dark ambiguities of flesh. My maker gave me but one command: mesh" (John Updike).

The preceding three biblical episodes can be taken as emblematic of the physical, psychological, and cultural evolution of human nature. And shame may be intimately connected with these three dimensions of human existence. First, shame has a basis in biology, as one of what James (1910) called the "coarse" emotions, in that it has a genetically inherited component (Scheff, 1987). Second, shame arises psychologically in situations of self-consciousness, seeing one's self from the viewpoint of others. Third, situations that produce shame, the labeling of shame, and the response to it show immense variation from one culture to another. Shame may be the most social of all emotions, since it functions as a signal of threat to the social bond.

The Old Testament contains many, many references to pride and shame but very few to guilt. The New Testament reverses the balance: There are many more references to guilt than to shame. One possible interpretation for this reversal is the difference between "shame cultures" and "guilt cultures." That is, the writers of the Old Testament were members of a completely traditional society in which shame was the major emotion of social control. Conversely, the writers of the New Testament were members of a society in transition to its current form, where the social control of adults involves guilt. This line of reasoning proposes external control through shame in traditional societies and internal control through guilt in modern societies (Benedict, 1946).

This book, however, offers a different explanation. I argue that the distinction between shame and guilt cultures is misleading since it assumes that shame states are infrequent in adults in modern societies. It is possible that the role of shame in social control has not decreased but has gone underground instead. In traditional societies, shame is openly acknowledged; the word itself is used frequently in everyday discourse. In modern societies, references to shame still appear frequently but in a disguised form.

As already suggested, there are many words and phrases that seem to be substitutes or euphemisms for shame or embarrassment. For example, we say, "It was an awkward moment for me." This statement usually refers to a feeling of embarrassment. It contains two movements that disguise emotion: *denial* of inner feeling and projection of it onto the outer world. *I* was not embarrassed; it was the *moment* that was awkward (Scheff, 1984). Our very language in modern societies conspires to hide shame from display and from consciousness. Traditional societies emphasize, or even exaggerate, shame; modern societies deny it. That is, the isolated form of alienation, and its concomitant denial of shame, was extremely rare in traditional societies. Like modern societies, traditional societies were a mixture of solidarity and alienation. But in traditional societies, alienation was likely to be in the form of engulfment.

Another issue concerns the meaning assigned to pride in the Old Testament. Virtually every reference places pride in a disparaging light. Perhaps the most familiar example occurs in Proverbs 16:18: "Pride goeth before destruction, and a haughty spirit before a fall." (In everyday usage, this quotation is often shortened to "Pride goeth before a fall.") A similar use occurs in 16:19: "Better it is to be of a humble spirit with the lowly than to divide the spoil with the proud." Many more similar examples could be cited.

This usage might be one of the sources of a contemporary inflection: that the word *pride* alone often carries a negative connotation. To escape that connotation, it is necessary to add a qualifier, e.g., *justified* pride. There might be less confusion if pride alone signified normal or justified pride. In this usage, it would be necessary to add a qualifier, e.g., *false* pride, to refer to the kind of pride so prominent in the Old Testament. There is a hint of this usage in the passage from Proverbs just cited: The kind of pride that leads to a fall is the kind that is marked by haughtiness. Perhaps false pride is unrelated to normal pride but to its antithesis, shame. Insolence and haughtiness may mask deep-seated feelings of inferiority, i.e., shame.

Other Historical Sources

False pride corresponds exactly to the meaning of the Greek word *hubris*, the kind of pride that leads certainly to nemesis, i.e., punishment by the gods. It appears that pride and shame played key roles in Greek thought since there were many shadings of each in classical Greek. In contrast to hubris, Aristotle depicted another kind of pride, which he saw as the supreme virtue, interest in honor above all else, a pride that means "greatness of soul." (For a fuller discussion of Aristotle's conception of pride as a virtue, and many other classical and medieval treatments of pride as well, see Payne, 1951.)

Among the various kinds of shame in the Greek language, the distinction between shame as disgrace (*aischyne*) and shame as modesty or shyness (*aidos*) has survived in all European languages except English:

	Disgrace	Modesty
Greek	*aischyne*	*aidos*
Latin	*foedus*	*pudor*
French	*honte*	*pudor*
Italian	*vergogna*	*pudore*
German	*Schande*	*Scham*

As already indicated, Schneider (1977) urged the importance of shame in this second meaning, "a sense of shame." This type of shame, especially in its root in the Greek word *aidos*, connotes not only modesty or shyness but also awe and reverence. Hume, in his eighteenth-century treatise on the passions ([1739] 1968), devoted considerable space to pride and shame. He noted the relationship of shame to humility and also distinguished between normal pride and false pride. (He called the latter "vanity.") A very precise analysis of Hume's approach to the emotions can be found in Taylor (1985).

Ovid ([7] 1955) depicted a relationship between shame and the stages of society in his four stages of the world. His first stage, the Golden Age, corresponded to the Garden of Eden, a world without fear and punishment. But this paradise was disturbed in the succeeding stages, until the last stage became an age of wickedness: "Every species of crime burst forth," and "shame [*pudor*], truth and honor took flight." This last passage suggests that wickedness involves, among other things, shamelessness, a loss of the sense of shame.

The connection among shamelessness, evil, and self-destruction was made quite explicit in the Greek myth of the Goddess Aidos, as told by Hesiod and others (Heller, 1984). In this myth Nemesis is the avenger of Aidos; that is, a shameless attack on decency, as personified by the goddess of shame, is tantamount to self-destruction. Surely the story of Hitler in Chapter 5 emblazons this idea on the universe.

The issue of shame first arose in the nineteenth century in a debate over blushing: Do dark-skinned persons blush? In a lengthy discussion of blushing and the emotions related to it, Darwin (1872, p. 309) concluded that dark-skinned races do indeed blush, that all humans do, and that blushing is a central feature of humanity: "Blushing is the most peculiar and most human of all expressions. ... Monkeys redden from passion, but it would require an overwhelming amount of evidence to make us believe that than any animal could blush." Darwin went on to state that blushing is caused by shame, the kind of shame that arises out of self-consciousness.

Approaches to a Concept of Shame

The idea that emotions can arise in seeing ourselves from the viewpoint of others, even if only in our imagination, plays a central role in Cooley's analysis (1922) of the nature of the self. He proposed that human consciousness is *social* in that we spend much of our lives "living in the minds of others" without realizing it. Self-monitoring from the viewpoint of others gives rise to self-regarding sentiments. Cooley emphasized two particular emotions that arise out of social self-monitoring: pride and shame. He implied that when we are adequately deferred to by others, we are in a state of normal pride. If we do not receive adequate deference, we enter a state of shame, as suggested in his discussion of the "looking-glass self" (1922, pp. 184–185):

> The thing that moves us to *pride* or *shame* is not the mere mechanical reflection of ourselves, but an imputed sentiment, the imagined effect of this reflection upon another's mind. This is evident from the fact that the character and weight of that other, in whose mind we see ourselves makes all the difference with our feeling. We are *ashamed* to seem evasive in the presence of a straightforward man, cowardly in the presence of a brave one, gross in the eyes of a refined one, and so on. We always imagine, and in imagining share, the judgments of the other mind. A man will boast to one person of an action—say some sharp transaction in trade—which he would be *ashamed* to own to another.

Cooley's statement suggests that pride and shame are virtually ubiquitous. We are accustomed to considering them unusual, arising infrequently, pride at rare occasions of triumph, shame at occasions of disgrace. But Cooley implied that we are virtually always in a state of either pride or shame. These ongoing states have such low visibility, however, that they are seldom noticed or mentioned. Cooley's approach suggests that normal pride and shame are existential states: They arise out of the innately social character of human nature. This idea anticipated Helen Lewis's (1971) approach to shame.

The work of Goffman (1959), who, like Cooley, was a sociologist, also implied a premier role for shame and embarrassment in human conduct. In his earliest approach, he only implied the role of emotion. He focused on a type of behavior, "impression management," which seemed to imply that a sense of shame determines most of our actions. His actors are obsessed with their image in the eyes of others, with the impression being made. His actors seem to constantly fear being seen negatively in the eyes of the other, which many writers have defined as the source of shame (as in Sartre, 1956).

In a later treatment of social interaction, Goffman (1967) made the role of shame more explicit, proposing that *embarrassment* (and anticipation of embarrassment) is a central ingredient of human contact. In presenting ourselves to others, we run the risk that our presentation will not be adequately accepted, that we will not receive the kind of response our presentation requires. His analysis concerned not just flagrant insults but also more subtle forms of disrespect, even a missed beat in the rhythm of conversation or an averted glance or direct stare held a fraction of a second too long. Goffman's work implies that emotion, particularly embarrassment, is the fuel that drives the social machine (Scheff, 1990).

The treatment of shame that has the largest scope is by Elias (1978; 1982) in his historical analysis of what he called the "civilizing process." In his historical studies, he traced changes in the development of personality with the onset of modern civilization. Like Max Weber, Elias gave great prominence to the development of rationality. Unlike Weber, however, Elias (1982, p. 292) gave equal prominence to changes in the threshold of shame: "No less characteristic of a civilizing process than 'rationalization' is the peculiar moulding of the drive economy that we call 'shame' and 'repugnance' or 'embarrassment'." Using excerpts from advice manuals, Elias outlined a theory of modernity. By examining instance after instance of advice concerning etiquette, especially table manners, body functions, sexuality, and anger, he suggested that a key aspect of modernity involved a veritable explosion of shame.

Although Elias's language is somewhat different, his analysis parallels mine. His central thesis is closely related to the one I earlier advanced (Scheff, 1990): Decreasing shame thresholds at the time of the breakup of rural communities and decreasing acknowledgment of shame had powerful consequences on levels of awareness and self-control. One of Elias's most telling examples is the kind of advice given in the nineteenth century about the education of girls (quoted in Elias, 1978, p. 180):

> Children should be left for as long as is at all possible in the belief that an angel brings the mother her little children. This legend, customary in some regions, is far better than the story of the stork common elsewhere. Children, if they really grow up under their mother's eyes, will seldom ask forward questions on this point ... not even if the

mother is prevented by a childbirth from having them about her. ... If girls should later ask how little children really come into the world, they should be told that the good Lord gives the mother her child, who has a guardian angel in heaven who certainly played an invisible part in bringing us this great joy. "You do not need to know nor could you understand how God gives children." Girls must be satisfied with such answers in a hundred cases, and it is the mother's task to occupy her daughters' thoughts so incessantly with the good and beautiful that they are left no time to brood on such matters. ... A mother ... ought only once to say seriously: "It would not be good for you to know such a thing, and you should take care not to listen to anything said about it." A truly well-brought-up girl will from then on feel shame at hearing things of this kind spoken of.

Elias's study suggests a way of understanding the social transmission of the taboo on shame and the social bond. In this quotation, the adult, the author von Raumer in this case, is not only ashamed of sex but is also ashamed of being ashamed and probably ashamed of the shame that he will arouse in his reader. His readers, in turn, probably reacted in a similar way, being ashamed, being ashamed of being ashamed, and being ashamed of causing further shame in the daughter. Von Raumer's advice was part of a social system in which attempts at civilized delicacy resulted in an endless chain reaction of unacknowledged shame. The chain reaction was both within persons and between them, a "triple spiral" (Scheff, 1990).

Elias's analysis is so broad and so trenchant that it takes us beyond the bounds of the present book. Here I focus on another kind of chain reaction, shame-anger spirals. Elias's analysis suggests the need for a future book, one that would explain the social transmission of patterns of shame management in terms of shame-shame spirals, just as I am explaining interminable conflict in terms of shame-anger spirals.

Certainly Elias (1978, p. 18) understood the significance of the denial of shame in the same way. Shame goes underground, leading to behavior that is outside of awareness and is compulsive:

Considered rationally, the problem confronting him [von Raumer] seems unsolved, and what he says appears contradictory. He does not explain how and when the young girl should be made to understand what is happening and will happen to her. The primary concern is the necessity of instilling "modesty" (i.e., feelings of shame, fear, embarrassment, and guilt) or, more precisely, behavior conforming to the social standard. And one feels how infinitely difficult it is for the educator himself to overcome the resistance of the shame and embarrassment which surround this sphere for him.

His analysis suggests some of the negative, indeed destructive, effects of secrets and secrecy in a way that directly contradicts Simmel's famous essay. Simmel seemed not to have noted the possible psychological and social effects of secrecy and silence. Understanding the dynamics of unacknowledged shame may lead to exact models of repression and precise and reliable methods of understanding behavior that is unconsciously motivated and compulsive. What does psychoanalysis, the discipline that owns the concepts of repression and the unconscious, have to say about shame?

At first sight, psychoanalytic theory gives the impression that shame has been all but ignored. Freud's primary emphasis was on anxiety and guilt. His approach implied that shame is "infantile" and "regressive." Schneider (1977) made a strong case that Freud was insufficiently sensitive to patients' desire to hide their secrets, their embarrassment, and their shame about their thoughts, feelings, and actions. He argued that Freud was shameless (in the sense of being disrespectful) in his relentless attack on what he thought of as the patients' "resistance" to knowing themselves. Schneider illustrated the problem with the way Freud mishandled the case of Dora, how Freud's irreverence toward a patient's sense of shame led him into a classic blunder. Perhaps the downplaying of shame is one of the key flaws in orthodox psychoanalytic theory and practice.

Although largely ignored in orthodox theory, shame emerges as central to several of the variant psychoanalytic theories. Adler's ([1907–1937] 1956) approach was centered on "feelings of inferiority," a phrase that seems to refer to shame. The theory pivots on a crucial phase in children's development when they need a secure bond with parents. Adler argued that children prefer love but that if it is unavailable to them, if they feel abandoned or rejected, their adult personality will develop in one of two ways. Either they will form an "inferiority complex"— that is, chronic feelings of shame (low self-esteem)—or they will manifest a "drive for power." Both paths may be interpreted in terms of chronic shame: the inferiority complex as *overt* shame, the drive for power as *bypassed* shame.

In Horney's (1950) approach to psychoanalysis, pride and shame play a central role. She termed the neurotic part of the personality the "false self," proposing that it is organized around what she called the "pride system." Her analysis implied that the pride in this system is false pride and that the system is driven by a sense of humiliation. She placed considerable emphasis on a particular *sequence* of events: honor, insult, and vindictiveness or revenge. Her analysis of this sequence anticipated my proposition that unacknowledged shame causes destructive aggression.

Piers and Singer (1953), Lynd (1958), and Tomkins (1963) also developed important analyses of shame and humiliation based in part on psychoanalytic ideas. In terms of my purpose here, however, the most important approach developed from psychoanalysis was that of Lewis. Her magnum opus, *Shame and Guilt in Neurosis* (1971), set forth the theory, method, and findings upon which much of this book is based.

Lewis's (1971) most important contribution was the discovery of *unacknowledged* shame, the kind of low-visibility emotion predicated by the work of Cooley and of Goffman. By patiently analyzing the transcripts of hundreds of psychotherapy sessions moment by moment, she demonstrated that patients were often in a state of shame. This state was virtually always overlooked by the therapist and the patient. Many of the patient's statements showed concern for the therapist's view of her: "I'm wondering how you are thinking about me after telling you all this." Both the manner and the content of these statements suggested shame states, but these were seldom made explicit.

Lewis's work suggests that shame is a haunting presence in psychotherapy that is usually hidden, disguised, or ignored by both patient and therapist. Returning to Cooley's conjecture about low-visibility pride, and Goffman's about embarrassment, we might infer that unacknowledged pride and shame are ubiquitous in all human encounters, not just in psychotherapy. This conjecture would explain why most therapists are unaware of pride and shame in therapy, even though they may turn out to be crucial elements in treatment: Like the patient and most other adults, the therapist is accustomed to ignoring the manifestations of these emotions.

Lewis also noted that shame usually occurred as a part of *sequence* of emotions. Her analysis of the foregoing patient's remark provided an example. The patient might have been imagining that he was seen in a negative way by the therapist: First a brief moment of shame was evoked, followed quickly by anger at the therapist, then, just as quickly, by guilt about the anger. This whole sequence might have occurred rapidly, lasting only fifteen or twenty seconds.

One important implication of Lewis's discovery of shame and shame-anger sequences concerns the emotions of guilt and resentment. Guilt is usually thought of as an elemental emotion like shame, and resentment is considered a form of anger. However, Lewis's analysis suggests that both these emotions are *shame-anger* variants: Guilt is a shame-anger sequence with the anger directed back at the self; resentment is a shame-anger sequence with the anger directed out at another. In this conception, guilt and resentment are isotopic variations of the basic shame-anger molecule. The sequential nature of this model suggests how guilt and resentment can last indefinitely as chains of emotional reactions to one's emotional reactions. That is to say, sequences of this kind can loop back on themselves, as when a patient feels ashamed for being so upset over "nothing," then angry because of the shame, and so on, ad infinitum. Lewis suggested that such sequences form "feeling traps," self-perpetuating chains of emotions. The idea of feeling traps may point toward a solution of the puzzle of lifelong guilt, resentment, and hatred (See Chapter 3). Finally, Lewis developed a method of detecting low-visibility shame in discourse. She noted that in a *context* that involved the patient seeing self from the therapist's point of view in a negative way, that both the patient's words and manner (tone of voice, loudness, speech static, self-interruptions, etc.) suggested a state of shame.

In her study of emotions in psychotherapy (1971), Lewis systematically rated cues for shame and anger, moment by moment, in audiotapes of several hundred sessions. For this purpose she used the Gottschalk-Gleser scale (1969) for rating emotions in verbal texts. Her method was to interpret each Gottschalk-Gleser rating in the situational context in which it occurred. Following Darwin, James,

McDougall, Cooley, and others, she defined the shame context as one in which the client seemed to be imagining self from the viewpoint of a negative other.

The method Lewis used combined system (Gottschalk-Gleser scales) and intuition (inferring context from client's comments, e.g., "You [the therapist] must think I'm crazy"). This method is a potent combination since it was systematic yet avoided decontexualizing the data. Her method was a form of what today is called "discourse analysis." It could be used to establish micro-macro linkage in discourse between individuals and between groups. In this way, it would provide instantiation (Giddens, 1984) at both micro- and macrolevels and trace the linkage between them.

Lewis's findings can be summarized under four headings. First, although her study detected many episodes of emotion, shame was by far the most prevalent, far outranking anger, grief, and fear, for example. Second, virtually all the shame episodes were *unacknowledged* by either party. That is, neither the patient nor the therapist commented on most of the shame states that Lewis's ratings revealed, or even seemed to be aware of them. At first sight, this finding was puzzling, since other emotions, such as anger and grief, were often acknowledged by one or both parties. How could a client's state of shame go by unnoticed by both client and therapist?

Third, Lewis suggested that adults in our society virtually always deny and disguise shame. Denial takes two forms, both of which disguise emotion from self and/or other. The first form is what she called *overt* shame. In this form, the client feels emotional pain to the point of slowing or disrupting thought and speech. There is usually fluster and unwanted physical symptoms such as blushing, sweating, or pounding heartbeat. The meaning of this syndrome is disguised, however, by misnaming. Instead of referring to shame, the client uses codewords such as "awkward," "uncomfortable," "insecure," "stupid," or "rejected." (A list of such words is provided by Gottschalk et al. 1969, in their "shame-anxiety" scale.) The meaning of the experience is disguised by a coded label, a form of denial.

Fourth, the second form is what Lewis referred to as *bypassed* shame. This form has characteristics opposite to those of overt shame: There is little pain and thought and speech are speeded up rather than slowed down. In this form, the individual appears to distract self from pain by rapid activity. Although behavior is fluent, it is slightly off key. This form of shame corresponds to Adler's ([1907–1937] 1956) drive for power, which he thought was a form of the inferiority complex (chronic shame). Although this behavior is goal oriented, it is as irrational as the behavior caused by overt shame; it is obsessive and compulsive. This finding is directly relevant to the theory of society as a moral order since it suggests a micro-macro model of conscience and consciencelessness.

Even in the most technical discussions of morality, conscience is taken to be an elemental; its meaning is never unpacked. For example, instead of explaining conscience, psychoanalytic theory merely gives it another name, the superego. Lewis's discovery of bypassed shame pointed toward an explicit model of conscience.

The connection between shame and conscience has been implied in many discussions. As already mentioned, two thousand years ago the poet Ovid connected the two: Wickedness involves shamelessness. Shame functions as an automatic pilot, a gyroscope. When it is bypassed, individuals and groups lose their moral direction, leading to conflict and anarchy.

Shame and the Social Bond

Shame and pride seem to be an almost continuous part of human existence not only in crises but also in the slightest of social contacts (Goffman, 1967). For example, we expect some slight acknowledgment of our presence even from strangers on the street. We recoil from feeling invisible to others, even if the others are unknown to us. In contact with intimates, even the most miniscule slackening of attention can be explosive. In a conversation with two of my friends, if one friend has only slightly more eye contact with my other friend than with me, I may become intensely upset all out of proportion to the difference. Each of us is acutely conscious of the amount and kind of attention we get from others. It seems that there is a virtually invisible thread connecting each of us to others. We are interdependent not only in the sense that our physical survival depends upon others to protect us from starvation and exposure but also in the emotional sense that we need to feel connected.

One way of making this point is to make an analogy between shame and fear, an emotion much better understood than shame. Just as fear automatically signals a threat to the safety of our *physical self* (our bodies), so shame automatically signals a threat to the safety of our *social self,* the person that we think we are and expect others to think that we are. We need to feel connected because the self is a social product, just as the body is a biological one.

Fear and shame are both automatic bodily signals; they are programmed by genetic inheritance (Brown, 1991). Babies do not need to learn either the fear or shame response since these emotions show up early in the first year of life. It makes sense that they are instinctive since each has survival value. Those individuals who are most sensitive to threats to their bodies or to their social bonds have a better chance of survival. The fear response signals the need for fight or flight; the shame response, to find out if one is being excluded or submerged in the group.

Since inclusion in a group without submersion is necessary for human survival, showing and detecting shame have survival value. Recent cross-cultural studies of politeness behavior also suggest the universality of shame: All known cultures provide elaborate means for protecting *face,* that is, protecting against embarrassment and humiliation (Brown and Levinson, 1987).

If shame is an innate, automatic bodily response, how is it that we see so little of it expressed by adults? I propose that in Western societies we learn to deny shame (to disguise and ignore it) from very early in childhood. To introduce the topic of denial, I return to the issue of the verbal expressions we use concerning shame and other painful feelings.

I have already mentioned the use of circumlocutions in the denial of shame. Suppression of references to emotion can occur in varying intensities, of which verbal evasions are one example. Acknowledgment means no suppression at all; it involves the direct naming and expression of an emotion. The verbal format is "I feel ashamed." However, verbal statement alone cannot acknowledge an emotion; it must also be felt and expressed. For example, in a genuine apology, one must not only say one is sorry; one must also feel sorry and show it (Tavuchis, 1991). Verbal expression without nonverbal expression, or the obverse, is the first step in suppression and denial.

Unfortunately, the concept of acknowledgment has yet to be sufficiently explained in the shame literature. Certainly its originator, Lewis (1971), had little to say about it. Acknowledgment is something of a weaselword, like the concept of "working through" in psychotherapy discourse: Everyone uses it, but no one has shown exactly what it means. Tavuchis's (1991) work precisely described the social dimension but did not sufficiently explore the requisite emotions. One way to begin is to be quite specific about the opposite of acknowledgment—suppression—of which there are several levels.

The first level of suppression is an indirect reference to the emotion of shame. The expression "It was an awkward moment for me" is an example. This level can be called the level of euphemism. We are familiar with such euphemisms in the babytalk parents use in referring to body parts and functions: wee-wee, poo-poo, and so on. These words are partial masks in that they evade the use of the actual names. But the level of suppression is not deep since the speakers are aware of the reference of these words.

A deeper level of suppression occurs when a word is used that disguises the reference not only to the listeners but also to the speaker. The word *hurt* for emotional pain in the way that James used it in the debriefing session provides an example. In using that word, James meant that in the face of Rosie's anger and contempt, he felt that Rosie was rejecting him as hopeless or worthless, which was a shame context. When he watched himself at this juncture in the debriefing session, what he saw were shame cues: fading smile, looking away, and shrinking down into his chair. The name he gave to the feelings he was expressing, however, was not shame but hurt.

James appeared unaware of his feelings at the time they occurred. In the debriefing session, he recognized that he was feeling an emotion, which he identified as hurt. His use of the word was not just a euphemism but an *encoding,* a concealing of the meaning of a message. In seeing his expression afterward, James realized that he was experiencing painful feelings but spoke of them in an encoded way. In the debriefing session, removed from the tension of the dispute, he still could not specify the actual emotion that he had felt.

The occasional use of words such as "upset" instead of "anger," and "hurt" or "insecurity" instead of "shame," is euphemistic; the speaker is aware of the feeling and the correct name for it. But much more often the level of suppression is deeper; the speaker who says "I felt uncomfortable" does not know that the feeling was embarrassment and may not recognize the greater appropriateness of that word even if someone else pointed it out. The concept of self-esteem seems to be an encoded reference to pride and shame. High self-esteem refers to a predominate experience of pride rather than shame.

The deepest level of suppression involves utter silence, with no references at all to a feeling, not even encoded ones. For example, in the nineteenth century, sexuality, especially women's sexuality, was surrounded by silence. And children can be shamed into silence and forgetting. Although the language in the von Raumer excerpt is no longer in vogue, many of the feelings remain the same. It appears that the majority of parents still remain silent about sexuality, even in the face of their children's increasing need for knowledge in this area. It is even possible that in some areas of knowledge, the depth of repression is increasing, as in attitudes toward death, anger, and dependence on others.

Shame as the Master Emotion

Shame seems to occupy a singular place among the emotions, and in social relationships. I call it the "master emotion" because it may have powerful psychological and social functions. First, for individuals, shame appears to be an automatic signal of the possibility of moral trespass. Conscience has a powerful and instinctive shame component (Scheff and Retzinger, 1991). This signal can be suppressed, but only at great cost. For most people, shame provides unmistakable signals of where they stand in the moral universe at any particular moment.

Second, normal shame signals the state of the social bond. Embarrassment and other shame signals warn us when self or other is feeling too close (exposed, violated) or too far (invisible, rejected). If these signals are suppressed and/or ignored, it may be almost impossible to know where we stand with another. Interaction takes on a stiff and formal character, with individuals flustered and self-conscious, which interferes with understanding and trust. Engulfment and isolation produce, and are produced by, the denial of shame. Recognition of shame and embarrassment signals in others is a recognition of their humanity: They are persons like ourselves.

It now seems likely that shame is a genetically inherited emotion that is a human universal. Since shame identifies threats to the social bond and to the integrity of the self, it makes sense that sensititivity to shame signals would be adaptive, that this kind of sensitivity would have survival value for the individual and the group.

Third, unacknowledged shame, a prevalent form of shame, can interfere with the discharge of painful emotions such as anger, fear, grief, and shame itself. Since shame is a self-conscious emotion, persons and groups may fall into traps of self-consciousness that interfere with normal biological, psychological, and social paths that allow the discharge of painful emotions. In the absence of unacknowledged shame, persons and groups with conflicting interests are always able to find the most beneficial or least destructive compromise. Unacknowledged shame paralyzes both the ability and desire to reach a compromise. For this reason, unacknowleged shame and alienation are the keys to understanding interminable impasses and quarrels (Scheff and Retzinger, 1991; Retzinger, 1991).

For these three reasons, pride and shame play an equal part with solidarity and alienation in determining the degree of social integration in a society, its capacity for cooperation and survival under stress, and its potential for fragmentation or violent disruption. Because we live in a highly individualized society, these matters have only recently come to our collective attention. Denial of shame goes hand in hand with denial of interdependence. An accurate and effective social science requires that shame and interdependence be brought into the light of day. These are the issues that will be addressed in the next chapter.

References

Adler, A. [1907–1937] 1956. *The Individual Psychology of Alfred Adler.* New York: Basic Books.

Benedict, R. 1946. *The Chrysanthemum and the Sword.* Boston: Houghton Mifflin.

Bowen, M. 1978. *Family Therapy in Clinical Practice.* New York: Jason Aronson.

Brown, D. 1991. *Human Universals.* New York: McGraw-Hill.

Brown, P., and S. Levinson. 1987. *Politeness Behavior: Some Universals in Language Usage.* Cambridge: Cambridge Univ. Press.

Cooley, C. H. 1922. *Human Nature and the Social Order.* New York: Scribner's.

Darwin, C. 1872. *The Expression of Emotion in Man and Animals.* London: John Murray.

Durkheim, E. [1897] 1952. *Suicide.* New York: Free Press.

Elias, N. 1978. *The History of Manners.* New York: Pantheon Books.

_____. 1982. *Power and Civility.* New York: Pantheon Books.

Giddens, A. 1984. *The Constitution of Society.* Berkeley and Los Angeles: Univ. of Calif. Press.

Goffman, E. 1959. *The Presentation of Self in Everyday Life.* Garden City, NY: Anchor Books.

_____. 1967. *Interaction Ritual.* Garden City, NY: Anchor Books.

Gottschalk, L., C. Wingert, and G. Gleser. 1969. *Manual of Instruction for Using the Gottschalk-Gleser Content Analysis Scales.* Berkeley and Los Angeles: Univ. of California Press.

Heller, E. 1984. *In the Age of Prose.* Cambridge: Cambridge University Press.

Horney, K. 1950. *Neurosis and Human Growth.* New York: Norton.

Hume, D. [1739] 1968. *Treatise on Human Nature. Vol. 2: The Passions.* Oxford: Clarendon Press.

James, W. 1910. *Psychology.* New York: Henry Holt.

Lewis, H. B. 1971. *Shame and Guilt in Neurosis.* New York: International Universities Press.

Lynd, H. 1958. *On Shame and the Search for Identity.* New York: Harcourt.

McDougall, W. 1908. *An Introduction to Social Psychology.* New York: University Paperbacks.

Ovid. [7] 1955. *Metamorphoses.* Bloomington: Univ. of Indiana Press.

Payne, R. 1951. *Hubris: A Study of Pride.* New York: Harper.

Piers, G., and M. Singer. 1953. *Shame and Guilt: A Psychoanalytic and Cultural Study.* New York: Norton.

Retzinger, S. M. 1991. *Violent Emotions: Shame and Rage in Marital Quarrels.* Newbury Park, CA: Sage.

Sartre, J. 1956. *Being and Nothingness.* New York: Philosophical Library.

Scheff, T. J. 1984 "The Taboo on Coarse Emotions." *Review of Personality and Social Psychology* 5: 146–169.

_____. 1987. "The Shame-Rage Spiral: Case Study of an Interminable Quarrel." In H. B. Lewis (ed.), *The Role of Shame in Symptom Formation.* Hillsdale, NJ: Erlbaum.

_____. 1990. *Microsociology: Discourse, Emotion, and Social Structure.* Chicago: Univ. of Chicago Press.

Scheff, T. J. and S. M. Retzinger. 1991. *Emotions and Violence: Shame and Rage in Destructive Conflicts.* Lexington, MA: Lexington Books.

Schneider, C. 1977. *Shame, Exposure, and Privacy.* Boston: Beacon Press.

Tavuchis, N. 1991. *Mea Culpa: A Sociology of Apology and Reconciliation.* Stanford: Stanford Univ. Press.

Taylor, G. 1985. *Pride, Shame, and Guilt.* Oxford: Clarendon Press.

Tomkins, S. 1963. *Affect/Imagery/Consciousness. Vol. 2: The Negative Affects.* New York: Springer.

Vico, G. [1744] 1968. *The New Science.* Ithaca, NY: Cornell University Press.

3

Alienation and Conflict:
A Theory of Interminable Conflict

What are the social conditions for conflict and cooperation between groups? In this chapter I propose a theory of alienation as an answer to this question. Cooperation between two groups requires a preponderance of solidarity both between and within each group: mutual identification and understanding. However, if alienation—that is, lack of mutual identification and lack of understanding (or misunderstanding)—prevails over solidarity, then there can be little cooperation. Alienation does not necessarily lead to conflict, however, since alienated groups and individuals can simply ignore each other rather than fight.

When does alienation lead to interminable conflict? I propose that alienation leads to lethal quarrels only under one condition: when it is *denied* by both parties. The denial of alienation is part of a package of wholesale denial of the elementary facts of a society, in particular, the denial of conflict and emotions. Wholesale denial seems to be an outgrowth of profound alienation: when the majority of the members of a group lack even one secure bond with another member (Scheff, 1990, Chap. 2). Under this condition, members are likely to deny their alienation, their emotions, and their own (and their group's) responsibility for any conflict in which they are involved.

Awareness of profound alienation of this kind is difficult in modern societies because, as already indicated, alienation takes two different forms: isolation (detachment from the group) and engulfment (detachment from self; Bowen, 1978). The ideology of extreme individualism idealizes isolation, thereby disguising and denying the need for social bonds. Given this ideology, isolation from others may be seen merely as a sign of personal independence and autonomy from the tyranny of the group.

Superpatriotism and other forms of blind loyalty idealize engulfment. In this form of alienation, the social bond is insecure because the individual has given up significant parts of the self in order to remain loyal to the group. A secure bond requires striking a balance between loyalty to the group and loyalty to the self, between interdependence and independence.

This kind of balance seems rare in modern societies. The most prevalent state may involve both kinds of alienation: engulfment *within* the group, isolation *outside* of it. In recent history, the rising tide of nationalism may represent this kind of alienation, which is *bimodal*. Social bonds within nations are insecure to the extent that they are based on blind loyalty (engulfment), mutual identification without mutual understanding, a false solidarity. The bond between nations suffers from isolation, leading to misunderstanding and lack of understanding. Rather than mutual identification, antagonism and rejection are the result.

Elias's (1987) discussion of the issue of alienation and solidarity between individuals (one component of bimodal alienation) was considerably simpler than those of Durkheim ([1897] 1952) and Bowen (1978) and those I used in my own earlier work. Elias referred merely to what he called the "I-we balance." This usage subsumes what Bowen and what I discussed earlier and Durkheim's distinction between egoistic and altruistic types of suicide. I think that egoism in Durkheim's sense means that a relationship is unbalanced toward the I, with more emphasis put on the individuals than the relationship, as does Bowen's concept of isolation. Similarly, altruism in Durkheim's sense means the opposite: The relationship is valued over the individual, as is also the case with Bowen's concept of engulfment. I find this usage not only simpler but also clearer and use it henceforth.

However, Elias's usage concerns only intragroup relationships. Since the concept of bimodal alienation concerns both intra- and intergroup relationships, it is necessary to introduce an intergroup dimension, the "us-them balance" (I am indebted to Joop Goudsblom for this happy formulation). The combinations of types of intra- and intergroup solidarity-alienation in the international system are rendered in Figure 3.1. In this formulation, there are two peaceful international systems, the medieval system, which is pacified but static, and the unalienated social system, which is both pacified and dynamic. All the other combinations result in conflict. The atomic case is like Hobbes's ([1651] 1987) image of the war of all against all. In the monolithic case, there is peace between groups but continuous conflict within them. The bimodal case is the most lethal of all since it pits group against group.

Alienation in itself does not lead to overt conflict when the alienated parties can ignore each other. Bimodal alienation generates conflict when it is consistently denied. Denial may generate intellectual and emotional tension to the point of massive outbreaks of collective hatred. To understand this process, let us review two recent developments in social science. The first involves the analysis of social solidarity and alienation, with emphasis on Bowen's (1978) approach to family

Intergroup	Intragroup		
	I **(isol.)**	**I-we** **(balanced)**	**We** **(engulfed)**
Us **(isolated)**	Atomized social system		Bimodal social system
Us-them **(balanced)**		Unalienated social system	
Them **(engulfed)**	Monolithic social system		Medieval social system

FIGURE 3.1 Group solidarity-alienation.

systems (Scheff, 1990). This approach calls attention to faulty communication tactics that both generate and signal alienation.

The second perspective is derived from the sociology of emotions, particularly the treatment of shame, anger, and aggression in Lewis (1971), Elias (1978, 1982), Scheff and Retzinger (1991), and Retzinger (1991). This approach describes the interaction between alienation and denial of emotions, focusing on the role played by unacknowledged shame both in signaling and generating alienation. The interplay between communication and emotion is diagrammed in Figure 3.2.

It has been difficult to formulate the role of bimodal alienation between and within groups because most social science discussions gloss over the complex interplay between self and society, between structure and process, between reason and emotion. A good example of such a gloss is provided by the idea of ethnocentrism. This concept was introduced into social science by Sumner (1911), who apparently borrowed it from Gumplowitz (1980). Sumner defined it as the practice of viewing all matters from the standpoint of one's own group. This usage is still current in social science, as in the discussions by Levine and Campbell (1971) and Staub (1989).

The concept of ethnocentrism masks several significant dimensions of social process and social structure. First, the concept is static, individualistic, and simplistic. As the term is usually used, it refers to a fixed attitude of individuals rather than one aspect of a complex social process. Second, it subsumes only the perceptual and cognitive aspects, excluding emotions. As did Sumner, current discussions assume that ethocentrism is a viewpoint or a set of beliefs, with little concern for the emotions that may also be present.

Current studies of ethnocentrism usually gloss over emotions, particularly pride and shame, in their analysis of the genesis of conflict. A distinction between pride and false pride is particularly important in understanding the causes of conflict. Most current discussions of "national pride," "race pride," or "group

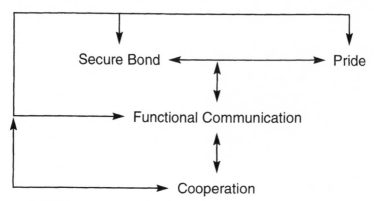

FIGURE 3.2a Social solidarity and cooperation.

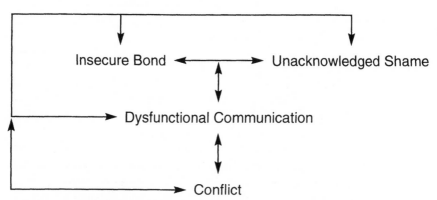

FIGURE 3.2b Alienation and conflict.

pride" confound pride with false pride, i.e., authentic, justified pride with a show of pride that is only a disguise. A person or group in a state of normal pride is usually not hostile or disparaging toward others. False pride, however, a mask for bypassed shame, generates hostility toward others.

Third, classic and current discussions usually do not attempt or are unable to assess the intensity of ethnocentric forces relative to other forces and therefore their importance in relationships between groups. This flaw is apparent in the doctrine widely held in current social science that ethnocentrism is universal. Although this doctrine may well be true, it avoids the issue that is central to this book: What are the conditions in a society that encourage runaway, exploding ethnocentrism? That is, when does ethnocentrism become the leading force in a society to the extent that other issues, even survival, seem to fade from consciousness? To explore this issue requires reviewing some basic ideas from family systems theory and from the sociology of emotions.

Family Systems and Emotions

I begin with communication tactics and alienation in family systems. Family members are alienated from their own conflicts to the extent that they are deceptive with each other and with self. To the degree that the basis of their own conflicts is invisible to them, they see these conflicts as exterior and constraining, as inevitable. This attitude toward conflict provides a strong link with Durkheimian theory: Warfare is a *social fact,* a social institution reaffirmed in the day-to-day organization of our civilization. To the extent that individuals and groups deny conflict and/or their own part in conflict, it will be seen as inevitable, a self-fulfilling prophecy.

Although family systems theory is immensely useful, a necessary component is missing if one is to understand interpersonal and intergroup conflict, the role of emotion sequences. In our theory (Scheff and Retzinger, 1991), we emphasize the way in which the emotion of shame is managed. Pride and shame are crucial elements in social systems. Pride signals and generates solidarity. In interaction, pride is signaled particularly by the play of the eyes, first looking into the eyes of the other, followed by looking away, then looking again, and so on. When both parties follow this sequence, the play of the eyes becomes a dance of interest and respect. The play of the eyes is only the most direct and obvious signal of pride and shame; it symbolizes a vast host of gestures that award or refuse deference and status (Goffman, 1967).

The emotion of shame can be directly acknowledged by referring to one's inner states of insecurity or feelings of separateness or powerlessness. Often shame goes unacknowledged to self and others. Unacknowledged shame takes two different forms. Overt shame is signaled by furtiveness; looking away or down predominates in the play of the eyes. In bypassed shame, one tries to outface the other, masking shame by staring directly at the other, a disrespectful gesture.

Acknowledging shame helps connect parties; admissions of feelings of weakness or vulnerability can build solidarity and trust (Lynd, 1958). Denying shame builds a wall between parties. If shame signals are disguised and/or ignored, both parties lose touch with each other. Pride and shame cues give instant indications of the "temperature" of the relationship. Pride means the parties are neither engulfed (too close), a we relationship, nor isolated (too far), an I relationship, but are emotionally and cognitively connected. Overt shame usually signals engulfment; bypassed shame, isolation.

Unacknowledged shame appears to be recursive; it feeds upon itself. To the extent that this is the case, it could be crucial in the causation of interminable conflict. If shame goes unacknowledged, it can loop back upon itself (being ashamed that one is ashamed) or co-occur with other emotions, such as grief (unresolved grief), fear (fear panics), or anger (humiliated fury). Unacknowledged shame seems to foil the biological and cultural mechanisms that allow for the expression and harmless discharge of these elemental emotions. If shame is absent or acknowledged, grief may be discharged by weeping under culturally appropriate conditions of mourning. But if shame is evoked by grief and goes unacknowledged, unending loops of emotions (shame-grief sequences) may occur. The individual will be unable to mourn.

If shame is evoked but is unacknowledged, it may set off a sequence of shame alternating with anger. (Shame-shame sequences are probably much more prevalent than shame-anger sequences. As indicated in Chapter 1, Elias's [1978, 1982] analysis of changes in advice manuals over the last five centuries implied that these sequences are a central core in the development of modern civilization to the extent that they occur in the socialization of children. But shame-shame sequences are beyond the scope of this book, which focuses on shame-anger.)

Anger may be interminable in the form of "helpless anger" or in the more explosive form, "humiliated fury." The shame-anger loop may be particularly central to destructive conflict. If one is in a shame state with respect to another, one route of denial is to become angered at the other, whether the other is responsible or not. That is, if one feels rejected by, insulted by, or inferior to another, denial of shame can result in a shame-anger loop of unlimited intensity and duration.

One difficulty in communicating this new theory is that emotions have virtually disappeared as creditable motives in modern scholarship. One would hardly know they existed from reading social science analyses of the causes of conflict. When references to emotions are made, they are likely to be abstract, casual, indirect, and brief. For example, emotions are sometimes invoked under the rubric of "nonrational motives," but with little attempt to specify what this category might contain.

The Emotional Sources of Vengeance

The identification of shame-anger sequences in the causation of conflict may help solve the problem of the causation of revenge. Although there is a very large literature on vengeance, it is almost entirely descriptive in nature. The largest literature is the anthropology of duels, feuds, and vendettas. Another very large literature concerns the revenge genre in world literature, especially in drama. A third, somewhat smaller, and less defined literature is on conflict in families.

These literatures testify to the way in which the revenge motive leads to interminable conflicts in human affairs and to the widespread popular appeal of dramatic portrayals of this motive. However, these literatures limit themselves to descriptions of the behavior involved. None offers substantive theories of the causation of revenge.

A similar paucity of explanations of revenge is also found in theories of human behavior. Surprisingly, there is only one book-length treatment of revenge in the entire human science literature, by Marongiu and Newman (1987). Although these authors attempted an explanatory formulation, it shed little light on the problem. Rather than ask the critical question—under which conditions does revenge occur and not occur?—this book offered a general and vague explanation for the existence of revenge in the human species.

Predictably, given the framing of the problem, one explanation Marongiu and Newman offered was genetic; they proposed an evolutionary account of the origins of revenge. They also offered what they thought of as a psychological alternative, drawing upon Freud's (1918) mythic formulation of the primal crime of the sons against the father. Freud's formulation was basically another version of the genetic explanation. He thought that the revenge motive might arise out of genetically driven sexual and aggressive instincts. For reasons already given, this approach is useless for explaining specific acts of vengeance. In this chapter I propose that a viable explanation should deal with emotions. In particular, my formulation suggests that emotional arousal leads to vengeful actions only if that arousal is denied.

Emotions as Explanations

There is a strong tradition in modern scholarship in the human sciences of ignoring emotions as causes. Even when words that reference intense emotions are used directly, the author often obscures the specifically emotional component by confounding it with a more rational motive. An example of the kind of confounding that frequently occurs involves the word *humiliation,* one of the most direct ways of referring to shame (Jervis, Lebow, and Stein, 1985, p. 140): "The dangers of *humiliation,* of conveying the appearance of weakness to real adversaries, were too great to permit acquiescence in the triumph even of apparent ones." The analyst was referring to the U.S. government's tendency to react to a Communist nation that is not dangerous (China) in the same way that it does to one that is dangerous (USSR).

At first glance one might think that the analyst is implying that governments, like individuals, sometimes act so as to avoid shame. Although a word is used that is clearly in the family of shame terms, invoking an emotional motive, the sentence also invokes the idea of avoiding not just shame but also the appearance of weakness. This is the modern lexicon of military strategy, of credibility and deterrence. By invoking this lexicon, the analyst managed to avoid the "nonrational" implications of his statement, i.e., the specifically emotional components of motivation. The entire literature on the strategy of deterrence is pervaded by exactly this confound.

In the narratives of these texts, such as the one by Jervis, Lebow, and Stein (1985), there are many references to humiliation, particularly in the discussions of concrete instances of conflict, as in the case of the Falklands War and the Israeli-Arab conflicts. But this word does not appear in the introduction, conclusion, or index. It does not have the conceptual status of a real motive. It is too useful to avoid entirely but too embarrassing to elevate to the status of a concept.

There are a number of psychoanalytically derived approaches to conflict that treat emotions directly. For the most part, however, following Freud, these studies have ignored shame. An example is provided by a study of the need to have enemies and allies (Volkan, 1988). This work focused on the inability to mourn (unresolved grief) in the exacerbation of conflict. Other studies emphasized the other two emotions that Freud recognized: anxiety and anger.

Shame is widely recognized as a cause of conflict in only one area: conflict and war among traditional peoples. Students of feuds and vendettas are apt to see humiliation and revenge as causal agents among premoderns, not "us," but "them." In an assessment of the causes of primitive warfare, Turney-High (1949, pp. 149–150, and 141–168) gave revenge pride of place:

> Revenge is so consistently reported as one of the principal causes of war that it requires detailed analysis. Why should the human personality yearn to compensate for its humiliation in the blood of enemies? The tension-release motive plays a part here: Revenge loosens the taut feeling caused by the slaying or despoiling of one's self, clan, tribe, nation. Even the hope for revenge helps the humiliated human to bear up, enables him to continue to function in a socially unfavorable environment. Fray Camposano wrote of the Mojos of southwestern Amazonia to Philip II of Spain that, "The most valiant were the most respected and their patience under injuries was only dissimulation for subsequent vengeance." Revenge, or the hope of revenge, restores the deflated ego, and is a conflict motive with which mankind must reckon with universally.

Even in this realm, explicit analysis of emotions as motives is an endangered species. Turney-High's explicitness occurred in a volume published in 1949. In the next generation of analysts, direct reference to avoidance of shame was considerably blunted.

In 1966, Peristiany edited a volume on feuds in Mediterranean society. It contained the word *shame* in its title and mentions in most of the chapters, but most of the authors carefully refrained from considering emotions to be motives. The exception was Pitt-Rivers' chapter on honor and social status. In his analysis of honor and shame (*vergüenza*) among the peasants of Andalusia, Pitt-Rivers (1966, p. 42) was direct to the point of bluntness about emotion words and their cognates: "As the basis of repute, honor and shame are synonymous, since shamelessness is dishonorable; a person of good repute is taken to have both, one of evil repute is credited with neither."

For most current scholars, the way in which Pitt-Rivers identified honor and shame as interchangeable parts of a larger cultural system of motivation and action would be utterly unacceptable. Pitt-Rivers must have been an entire generation older than the other contributors, putting him in the same cohort as the equally blunt Turney-High.

In recent treatments of primitive warfare (Riches, 1986; Turner and Pitt, 1989; Haas, 1990), references to emotions have all but disappeared. Even more indirect references, e.g., to actions such as revenge that are closely related to emotional motives, are less frequent and more dispersed. This is not to say that analysts completely avoid the consideration of emotional motives. What has happened is that such motives are treated distantly and briefly and in terms that are more diffuse: prestige, face saving, and status competition. The vagueness of these terms facilitates the kind of confounding already mentioned: Emotions lead only a shadow life these days. Shame, particularly, has dropped out of the discussion, along with other emotions and personal motives. Lust for possessions or power is seen as real; for honor, unreal.

It is difficult to locate the exact time in which shame and humiliation dropped out of the lexicon of respectable motives. Strong decrements seemed to occur in the two eras just preceding and during the two world wars. In the nineteenth century, it was still possible to name "national honor" as a reason for going to war, as in the origins of the Spanish-American War. But by the beginning of World War I, this kind of motive no longer had full legitimacy. Even in pre–World War I France, where there was still much public talk of the honor, glory, and triumph associated with war, revenge was seen as too coarse a motive to countenance openly.

This timing might correspond to the lowering trajectory of shame thresholds traced by Elias (1978, 1982), which he proposed to be one of the key characteristics of modernity ("us"). Increasingly, as shame thresholds and open acknowledgment of shame decrease, social scientists, like most others in our civilization, are too ashamed of emotions to give them serious attention as causal elements.

This one change may have wrought havoc with our understanding of human motives in general and specifically with analyses of the causes of conflict. Governments and their analysts seem forbidden to talk or even think about emotional motives. Instead, duplicity, indirection, and silence reign. If we cannot talk openly about the emotional causes of conflict, we may be trapped in the process of embarrassing ourselves to death.

The stance of the analysts of the actions of governments is virtually always that of the isolated, bypassed style: Emotional motives are mentioned only casually and distantly (e.g., prestige) or not at all. None of the many governmental and scholarly discussions of the strategy of deterrence even acknowledges the possibility that there might be an emotional, "nonrational" component in this strategy. Emotions have disappeared not only from the statement and actions of governments but also from the writings of most scholars. Humiliated fury is not the creditable, respectable motive that power, territory, or other objectified motives are. As Emerson said, "Things are in the saddle; they ride humankind." Objectification sets the stage for and reflects alienation between persons and between nations.

Pride and Shame

The psychoanalytic idea of repression may be helpful in understanding defenses against inadequate bonding. If the ideology of the self-sufficient individual is a defense against the pain of threatened bonds, what is being repressed is the *idea* of the social bond. Freud, however, argued that repression concerns not only ideas but also the *feelings* that accompany them. He thought that repression could be lifted only if both idea and emotion were expressed. If modern societies repress the idea of the social bond, what are the associated feelings that are also repressed?

I follow the lead of Cooley (1922), who implied that pride and shame are the primary social emotions. These two emotions have a signal function with respect to the social bond. In this framework, pride and shame serve as intense and automatic signs of the state of a system otherwise difficult to observe. As will be indicated in Chapter 5, secure social bonds were unknown to Hitler and also seem to have been in short supply in the society in which he grew up. To understand how this situation might have led to implacable vengefulness, I once more review how emotions can cause continuous conflict.

Unending Emotions

I propose that unacknowledged alienation leads to interminable conflict. Like Watzlawick et al. (1967), I argue that some conflicts are unending, any particular quarrel being only a link in a continuing chain. What causes interminable conflict?

My theory advances two forms of interminable conflict: the quarrel and the impasse. Both forms grow out of unacknowledged shame. Shame is pervasive in conflictful interaction but is invisible to interactants (and to researchers) unless Lewis's (or Gottschalk et al.'s [1969]) approach is used. I connect the two forms of conflict with the two forms of unacknowledged shame; quarrels with the bypassed form, impasses with the overt, undifferentiated form.

The two forms of shame are polar opposites in terms of thought and feeling. Overt shame involves painful feeling with little ideation; bypassed shame, rapid thought, speech, or behavior but little feeling. The two forms correspond to a distinction in Adler's ([1907–1937] 1956) theory of personality: Children lacking a secure bond at critical junctures respond in two different ways, either with an "inferiority complex" (chronic overt shame), or a drive to power (behavior masking bypassed shame). (My discussion in Chapter 4 will show how the drive-for-power, bypassed-shame formulation fits Hitler's personality.) Lewis's analysis paralleled Adler's but also represented an immense advance over it. Unlike Adler, Lewis described observable markers for the theoretical constructs and specified the causal sequence, the unending spiraling of emotion in feeling traps.

Overt shame is marked by furtiveness, confusion, and bodily reactions: blushing, sweating, and/or rapid heartbeat. One may be at a loss for words, with fluster or disorganization of thought or behavior, as in states of embarrassment. Many of the common terms for painful feelings appear to refer to this type of shame or combinations with anger: feeling peculiar, shy, bashful, awkward, funny, bothered, or miserable; in adolescent vernacular, being freaked, bummed, or weirded out. The phrases "I felt like a fool" or "I felt like a perfect idiot" may be prototypic.

Bypassed shame is manifested as a brief, painful feeling that usually lasts less than a second and is followed by obsessive and rapid thought or speech. A common example: One feels insulted or criticized. At that moment (or later in recalling it), one might experience a jab of painful feeling (producing a groan or wince), followed immediately by imaginary but compulsive, repetitive *replays* of the offending scene. The replays are variations on a theme: how one might have behaved differently, avoiding the incident or responding with better effect. One is obsessed.

Lewis (1971) referred to the internal shame-rage process as a feeling trap, as "anger bound by shame" or "humiliated fury." Kohut's (1971) concept, "narcissistic rage," appears to be the same affect since he viewed it as a compound of shame and rage. Angry that one is ashamed, or ashamed that one is angry, one might then be ashamed to be so upset over something so "trivial." Such anger and shame are rarely acknowledged, difficult to detect and dispel. Shame-rage spirals may be brief, a matter of minutes, but can also last for hours, days, or a lifetime as bitter hatred or resentment.

Brief sequences of shame-rage may be quite common. Escalation is avoided through withdrawal, conciliation, or some other tactic. In this book a less common type of conflict is described. Watzlawick et al. (1967, 107–108) called it "symmetrical escalation." Since such conflicts have no limits, they may have lethal outcomes. In this theory, unacknowledged shame is the cause of revenge-based cycles of conflict (this formulation was anticipated in the work of Geen [1968] and Feshbach [1971]). Shame-rage may escalate continually to the point that a person or a group can be in a permanent fit of shame-rage, a kind of madness.

Studies of Shame and Aggression

The theory outlined here is supported by several exploratory studies. Katz (1988) analyzed descriptions of several hundred criminal acts: vandalism, theft, robbery, and murder. In many of the cases, Katz (1988, p. 8) found that the perpetrator felt humiliated, committing the crime as an act of revenge. In some of the cases the sense of humiliation was based on actual insults: "[A] ... typical technique [leading to a spouse being murdered] is for the victim to attack the spouse's deviations from the culturally approved sex role. ... For example, a wife may accuse her husband of being a poor breadwinner or an incompetent lover. ... Or the husband may accuse his wife of being 'bitchy,' 'frigid,' or promiscuous."

In other cases it was difficult to assess the degree to which the humiliations were real or imagined. Whatever the realities, Katz's findings support the model of the shame-rage feeling trap. In his analysis of the murder of intimates, he said (1988, p. 11) "The would-be-killer must undergo a particular emotional process. He must transform what he initially senses as an eternally humiliating situation into a blinding rage." Rather than acknowledging his or her shame, the killer masks it with anger, the first step into the abyss of the shame-rage feeling trap, which ends in murder. Katz reported similar, although less dramatic, findings with respect to the other kinds of crimes he investigated.

One issue that Katz's study did not address is the conditions under which humiliation is transformed into blind rage. Since not all humiliations lead to blind rage, there must be some ingredient that is not indicated in Katz's cases. Studies of family violence by Lansky suggested this extra ingredient. To lead to blind rage, the shame component in the emotions that are aroused must be unacknowledged. Lansky has published three papers on family violence.

The first (1984) described six cases; the second (1987) investigated four; the third (1989) analyzed one session with a married couple. In most of the cases, he reported similar emotional dynamics: violence resulted from the insulting manner that both husbands and wives took toward each other. Although some insults were overt, in the form of cursing, open contempt, and disgust, most were covert, in the form of innuendo or double messages.

Underhanded disrespect gave rise to unacknowledged shame, which in turn led to anger and violence in the way predicted by Lewis. It was difficult for the participants to respond to innuendo and double messages; these forms of communication confused them. Instead of admitting upset and puzzlement, participants answered in kind. The cycle involved disrespect, humiliation, revenge, counter-revenge, and so on, ending in violence.

The way in which both spouses seemed to be unaware of the intense shame that their behavior generated can be illustrated in one of the cases (Lansky, 1984, pp. 34–35; emphasis added):

> A thirty-two year old man and his forty-six-year-old wife were seen in emergency conjoint consultation after he struck her. Both spouses were horrified, and the husband agreed that hospitalization might be the best way to start the lengthy treatment that he wanted. As he attempted to explain his view of his difficult marriage, his wife disorganized him with repeated humiliating comments about his inability to hold a job. These comments came at a time when he was talking about matters other than the job. When he did talk about work, she interrupted to say how immature he was compared to her previous husbands, then how strong and manly he was. The combination of building up and undercutting his sense of manliness was brought into focus. As the *therapist* commented on the process, the husband became more and more calm. ... After the fourth session, he left his marriage and the hospital for another state and phoned the therapist for an appropriate referral for individual therapy. On follow-up some months later, he had followed through with treatment.

The disguising of the wife's humiliation of the husband in this case was not through innuendo since her disparagement was overt. Her shaming tactics were disguised by her technique of alternately praising her husband, by stating how "strong and manly" he was, and then cutting him down. Perhaps she confused herself with this tactic as much as she did her husband.

Lack of awareness of shaming and shame can be seen in Lansky's (1989) report of a conjoint session with a violent man and his wife. In this session, Lansky indicated that the wife was dressed in a sexually provocative way and that her bearing and manner were overtly seductive toward the interviewer. Yet neither spouse acknowledged her activity, even when the interviewer asked them whether the wife was ever seductive toward other men. Although both answered affirmatively, their answers concerned only past events. The lack of comment on what was occurring at that very moment in the interview is astounding. It would seem that blind rage requires not only shaming and shame but also blindness toward these two elements.

The relationship between collective violence and unacknowledged shame was suggested by a recent analysis of the Attica riots (Scheff, Retzinger, and Ryan, 1989). The violence of the guards toward the inmates began with a series of events that the guards perceived as humiliating: Without consulting the guards, a new warden intent on reform increased the rights of the prisoners, which resulted in a series of incidents with prisoners that guards experienced as humiliating. Since the guards did not acknowledge their humiliation, their assault on the prisoners followed the sequence predicted by the Lewis theory: insult, unacknowledged shame, rage, and aggression.

This formulation does not discount the importance of the topic of conflict, be it scarce resources, cultural differences, or any other issue. But this formulation argues that in the absence of unacknowledged shame, human beings are resourceful enough to be able to find a compromise to any dispute that is most beneficial to both parties or least harmful. If shame is evoked in one or both parties, however, and is not acknowledged, then the content of the dispute becomes less important than the hidden emotions, which take over. Unacknowledged shame could be the basis of what Goffman (1967) called "character contests," conflicts in which the topic of dispute becomes subordinate to the issue of "face."

Conclusion

The theory outlined here may provide a solution to the problem of interminable and destructive conflict. This theory can be summarized in terms of three propositions:

1. Bimodal alienation (engulfment within and isolation between groups) inhibits cooperation both within and between groups. Understanding,

trust, and cooperation become increasingly difficult to the extent that social bonds are insecure.

2. Bimodal alienation leads to interminable conflict if, and only if, alienation and its accompanying emotions are denied. This proposition may be true independently of the gravity of the differences in interests between the two groups. That is, the most beneficial or the least harmful compromise on differences of interests can be found if alienation is acknowledged.

3. The denial of alienation generates an emotional process that leads to escalation of conflict, a triple spiral of shame-rage between and within parties to a conflict. Acknowledgment of alienation and shame deescalates conflict, independently of the differences of interests between the parties.

This formulation has a number of advantages over existing ones. Rather than being based on the assumption that groups are made up of isolated indivudals, it assumes a structure/process composed of social relationships. This formulation is not static since it proposes that the degree of conflict at any moment is based on the state of social bonds within and between the contending parties at that moment. The formulation is exceedingly complex since it suggests an analysis of solidarity and alienation in terms of actual social relationships between and within the parties to a conflict.

Unlike many theories of conflict, this one offers a description of the causal chain that links social and psychological conditions to the generation of conflict. Communication practices that serve to deny alienation and emotion generate spirals in which emotions escalate to the point of intolerable tension, explaining the origin of "war fever" and other highly irrational behaviors by individuals and groups.

Finally, this theory is potentially testable since it provides detailed descriptions of its elemental components: alienation and emotion. For this reason, it might be seen as a "grounded theory" (Glaser and Strauss, 1967). In a study of videotapes of game shows, Retzinger and I (1991) demonstrated that markers of solidarity and alienation can be rated systematically and that alienation interferes with the ability of contestants to cooperate and, therefore, to win.

In a work on marital quarrels, Retzinger (1991) demonstrated that shame and anger can be systematically rated in videotape recordings. Her findings in each of four quarrels suggest that unacknowledged shame always precedes, rather than follows, the disrespectful anger that leads to escalation. At an interpersonal level, her work supports Simmel's conjecture that separation leads to conflict rather than the other way around. In the next two chapters I will apply this theory to conflict at the level of world systems, the causes of World Wars I and II.

References

Adler, A. [1907–1937] 1956. *The Individual Psychology of Alfred Adler.* New York: Basic Books
Bowen, M. 1978. *Family Therapy in Clinical Practice.* New York: Jason Aronson.

Cooley, C. H. 1922. *Human Nature and the Social Order*. New York: Scribner's.

Coser, L. A. 1956. *The Functions of Social Conflict*. Glencoe, IL: Free Press.

Durkheim, E. [1897] 1952. *Suicide*. New York: Free Press.

Elias, Norbert. 1972. *What Is Sociology?* London: Hutchison.

_____. 1978. *The History of Manners*. New York: Pantheon Books.

_____. 1982. *Power and Civility*. New York: Pantheon Books.

_____. 1987. *Involvement and Detachment*. Oxford: Basil Blackwell.

Freud, S. 1918. *Totem and Taboo*. New York: Moffat and Yard.

Ferguson, B. 1988. *The Anthropology of War*. New York: Occasional Paper of the Herman Guggenheim Foundation.

Feshbach, S. 1971. "The Dynamics and Morality of Violence and Aggression." *American Psychologist* 26: 281–292.

Geen, R. G. 1968. "Effects of Frustration, Attack, and Prior Training in Aggressiveness upon Aggressive Behavior." *Journal of Personality and Social Psychology* 9: 316–321.

Glaser, B. and A. Strauss, 1967. *The Discovery of Grounded Theory*. Chicago: Aldine.

Goffman, E. 1967. *Interaction Ritual*. Garden City, NY: Anchor Books.

_____. 1971. *Relations in Public*. New York: Harper.

Gottschalk, L., C. Wingert, and G. Gleser, 1969. *Manual of Instruction for Using the Gottschalk-Gleser Content Analysis Scales*. Berkeley and Los Angeles: Univ. of California Press.

Gumplowicz, L. 1980. *Outline of Sociology*. New Brunswick, NJ: Transaction Books.

Haas, J. 1990. *The Anthropology of War*. Cambridge: Cambridge Univ. Press.

Hobbes, T. [1651] 1987. *Leviathan*. Harmondsworth: Penguin Books.

Jervis, R., N. Lebow, and J. Stein, 1985. *Psychology and Deterrence*. Baltimore: Johns Hopkins Univ. Press.

Katz, J. 1988. *The Seductions of Crime*. New York: Basic Books.

Kohut, H. E. 1971. "Thoughts on Narcissism and Narcissistic Rage." In *The Search for the Self*. New York: International Universities Press.

Lansky, M. 1984. "Violence, Shame, and the Family." *International Journal of Family Psychiatry* 5: 21–40.

_____. 1987. "Shame and Domestic Violence." In D. Nathanson (ed.), *The Many Faces of Shame*. New York: Guilford Press.

_____. 1989. "Murder of a Spouse: A Family Systems Viewpoint." *International Journal of Family Psychiatry* 10: 159–178.

Levine R. T., and D. T. Campbell. 1971. *Ethnocentrism: Theories of Conflict*. New York: Wiley.

Lewis, H. B. 1971. *Shame and Guilt in Neurosis*. New York: International Universities Press.

Lynd, H. 1958. *Shame and the Search for Identity*. New York: Harcourt.

Marongiu, P., and G. Newman. 1987. *Vengeance: The Fight Against Injustice*. Towota, NJ: Rowman and Littlefield.

Peristiany, J. 1966. *Honor and Shame in Mediterranean Societies*. Chicago: Univ. of Chicago Press.

Pitt-Rivers, J. 1966. "Honor in Traditional Societies." In J. Peristiany (ed.), *Honor and Shame in Mediterranean Societies*. Chicago: Univ. of Chicago Press.

Retzinger, S. M. 1991. *Violent Emotions: Shame and Rage in Marital Quarrels*. Newbury Park, CA: Sage.

Riches, D. 1986. *The Anthropology of Violence*. Oxford: Basil Blackwell.

Scheff, T. J. 1990. *Microsociology: Discourse, Emotion, and Social Structure*. Chicago: Univ. of Chicago Press.

Scheff, T. J., and S. M. Retzinger, 1991. *Emotions and Violence: Shame and Rage in Destructive Conflicts.* Lexington, MA: Lexington Books.

Scheff, T., S. Retzinger, and M. Ryan. 1989. "Crime, Violence and Self-Esteem: Review and Proposals." In A. Mecca, N. Smelser, and J. Vasconcellos (eds.), *The Social Importance of Self-Esteem.* Berkeley and Los Angeles: Univ. of California Press.

Simmel, G. 1950. *The Sociology of Georg Simmel.* Glencoe, IL: Free Press.

———. 1955. *Conflict and the Web of Group-Affiliations.* New York: Free Press.

Staub, E. 1989. *The Roots of Evil: Origins of Genocide.* New York: Cambridge Univ. Press.

Sumner, W. G. 1911. *Folkways.* Boston: Ginn.

Tavuchis, N. 1991. *Mea Culpa: A Sociology of Apology and Reconciliation.* Stanford: Stanford Univ. Press.

Turner, P., and D. Pitt. 1989. *The Anthropology of War and Peace.* Granby, MA: Bergin and Garvey.

Turney-High, H. H. 1949. *Primitive War.* Columbia: Univ. of South Carolina Press.

Volkan, V. 1988. *The Need to Have Enemies and Allies.* Northvale, NJ: Jason Aronson.

Watzlawick, P., J. H. Beavin, and D. Jackson. 1967. *The Pragmatics of Human Communication.* New York: Norton.

PART TWO

Applications

4

The World Social System: The Origins of World War I

In this chapter I argue that the immediate causes of war lie in the alienated relationships that are endemic in our civilization. These causes are equally present in the smallest unit of sociation—the family system—and in the relations between nations. The patterns of secrecy, deception, and self-deception that prevail in the relationships of family members can also be found in parallel forms in the relationships among nations. Drawing upon family systems theory and the sociology of emotions, I outline a theory that describes how alienation and unacknowledged shame produce wars. To illustrate this theory, I apply it to a hotly contested problem, the origins of World War I.

In claiming an isomorphism between interpersonal and international relations, I realize that I challenge an article of faith of modern social science: that structure and process at the societal level are fundamentally different from those at the level of persons; society, as Durkheim ([1912] 1954) claimed, is a reality sui generis. Although I agree that societal relationships are in some ways different from interpersonal ones, I propose that they are also in other ways the same. I show parallels between the communication tactics and emotion that occur in families and in relations between nations.

In classical political theory, as in Machiavelli ([1431] 1988), the parallel between personal and political relations was taken as a truism. With the rise of nationalism and the nation-state, however, an opposing presumption appeared: that reasons of state were utterly different from those of individuals and mere social groups and were sacrosanct. This presumption still bedevils political theory since it privileges one social formation at the expense of all others. Kissinger's (1957) study of the maneuvers of Metternich can be taken as a representative example of the fallacies that result from this presumption.[1]

---

1. I am indebted to Edward Muir for the ideas in this paragraph.

For a discipline to retain its cutting edge, that discipline must maintain a balance between accepting the established consensus and challenging it. A scholar need not challenge every tenet in a discipline or accept every tenet on faith. Maintaining a judicious balance between skepticism and faith is a demanding but necessary task, if a scholar's work is to be more than a mere exercise.

Eliot observed that one "cannot inherit a tradition; it must be acquired by hard labor." In modern social science there is a tendency to evade that hard labor by conforming to the established tenets on faith, creating an imbalance. As my contribution toward decreasing the imbalance, in this chapter I challenge not one article of faith but two. The first has already been mentioned: the conjecture that societal process is fundamentally different from that between persons, a tenet of theory. The second is a substantive tenet: Germany's war guilt. The problem of the origins of World War I is recognized in the disciplines of history and political science to be of considerable scope and complexity, one of the principal conundrums, like the fall of Rome. Kennan (1979, p. 4) put the matter very well:

> Were we not *in the face of some monstrous miscalculation—some pervasive failure to read correctly the outward indicators on one's own situation ... ? Must not the generation of 1914 have been the victim of certain massive misunderstandings, invisible, of course, to themselves but susceptible of identification today ... ? Was there not a possibility that if we could see how they went wrong, if we could identify the tendencies of mass psychology that led them thus astray, we might see where the dangers lay for ourselves in our attempt to come to terms with some of the great problems of public policy of our own day?*

Authors also acknowledge that in spite of a very large number of attempts, no one has come even close to solving this problem. Consensus reigns on both these points. Yet at the same time, the great majority of researchers seem to tacitly agree that the solution is to be found in the analysis of the aims and actions of one of the nations who fought the war: Germany. To be sure, there are minority positions, one being taken by those researchers who propose that France played a vital role in instigating the war. Nevertheless, it is stated or assumed in a sizable majority of studies that the basic causes of the war are to be found in German militarism and imperialism.

In this chapter, I challenge the assumption that Germany was the sole culprit. I claim that all five of the major powers were *equally* responsible for the onset of the war: Germany and Austria-Hungary (the Central Powers) and France, Russia, and England (the Allies). This argument is a familiar one in family systems analysis: In interminable family conflict, it is argued, all members contribute more or less equally to neverending discord. I propose that the onset of World War I was mutually and jointly caused by the five major combatants. To argue that one or the other of the nations was most culpable is to mistake the *part* for the *whole* (Scheff, 1990): These nations had created a system of alienated relationships between persons and between groups. Both as individuals and groups, they denied their own responsibility, creating through this maneuver their own entrapment.

Most studies of war fall into one of two camps; either they evade/ignore the problem of causation, or they assume that causes are to be found in some discrete event, person, or nation. My argument contradicts this assumption. I propose that our civilization is a *system*, one that produces the character of the actors and the organization of communication. This system is not directly visible to its members; if allowed to function uninterrupted, it will produce intermittent wars in the same way that it produces shoddy consumer goods, prisons, and ecological disaster. By becoming aware of the system, perhaps we can escape its imperatives.

The alienation between France and Germany that led to two world wars can be represented dynamically in terms of unacknowledged shame. Alienation, threat to a bond, causes and is caused by shame. Humiliated fury by the French toward the Germans after France's defeat in 1871 was the prime mover in the part that France played in starting World War I. Humiliated fury by the Germans toward the French and their allies after Germany's defeat in 1918 created Hitler's appeal to the Germans, which led to the World War II (Chapter 5). Since the cues to these emotions are clear in discourse, they allow us to assess the state of the bond in every message exchanged between disputants.

Conflicts of interest and outlook between the major powers do not seem compelling as a cause of World War I. Unlike the situation prior to World War II, where there were intractable differences between the worldviews of the Allied and Axis powers, in 1914 the differences of outlook were relatively minor. Although there were many, they seem in retrospect all capable of having been sorted out by negotiation.

Russell (1916), who was jailed because of his opposition to the war, provided a clue to the social-emotional causes: He called it a "vanity war." Goffman's (1967) idea of character contests strikes a similar chord. In an alienated state, individuals and groups can be quickly humiliated to the point that irrational emotions determine behavior. The dynamics of the headlong rush to war can be understood in terms of unacknowledged shame.

It is possible that other emotions are involved in irrational destruction. It seems to me that the nations of Europe had good reason to fear each other: Fear as well as shame might generate rage, as Gaylin (1984) suggested. Anxiety is another emotion that is frequently evoked to explain irrational behavior. In Chapter 6 I will further discuss the possibility of studying fear and anxiety as causes of conflict. In this chapter I limit my analysis of emotions to shame and anger.

The Origins of World War I

Figure 4.1 shows the major nations involved in World War I. I have placed England at the equipoise because of its last-minute entry into the war. To understand the origins of this war, let us first consider the relationship between France and Germany and between these two countries and the other three in the years prior to the war. Germany and England were by far the most powerful and stable

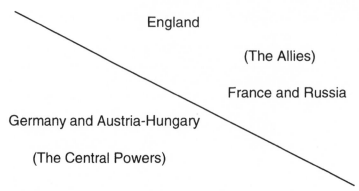

England

(The Allies)

France and Russia

Germany and Austria-Hungary

(The Central Powers)

FIGURE 4.1 The major nations involved in the origins of World War I.

of the group, with France next, followed by Russia and Austria-Hungary. These last two countries were particularly weak and unstable; Russia because it was vast, underdeveloped, led by an incompetent elite, and riven by political and ethnic animosities; Austria-Hungary because it was smaller (although more developed) and in a situation similar to Russia's. The onset of World War I can be seen as the way in which the weakest members of the family manipulated the strongest.

This manipulation could have occurred only in a system of dysfunctional communication tactics and repressed emotions. Unacknowledged shame was transformed into self-righteous anger. Deception, self-deception, and secrecy allowed these emotions to generate an irrational and unnecessary bloodbath. My analysis sugests that prior to the onset of World War I, the relationships among the five principal nations were dysfunctional. In the case of England, we now know that within that nation, secrecy obtained between the foreign minister and the rest of the nation; vital information was withheld even from the members of the cabinet.

Prior Studies

To show the power of a systems analysis of the origins of war, I review and reassess a standard work, the chapter on World War I in John Stoessinger's (1990) study of the causes of modern wars. This study is a useful one for my purposes for several reasons. First, it represents the majority position on World War I; Stoessinger made a careful analysis that seemed to incriminate Germany. Second, his study is stronger than most of the others in two ways. Stoessinger based his core argument on an analysis of some of the discourse that took place among Germany, Russia, and England immediately prior to the onset of the war. Such an approach makes possible a part/whole analysis of social systems since it offers data at both the level of individuals and of groups. Social structure and emotion ride upon manner and implicature; they are deeply embedded in the context and in the details of specific events. Stoessinger's approach was also comparative and analytic: His chapter on the onset of World War I was the first in several similar analyses of the causes of other modern wars.

Stoessinger's study stands out because it combines an interest in the details of the particular case with a comparison with other cases. Most attempts to understand the causes of war are either particularizing and descriptive or abstract and generalizing, but not both. Either type of specialized study precludes part/whole analysis. Stoessinger's approach allows one to see further than he did by standing on his shoulders and those of others who have attempted to deal with this problem.

Of the many efforts, the one most frequently praised is that of Joll (1984). Although balanced and temperate, this work was also abstract and descriptive. A review of the various earlier studies, on which most current scholarship is based, can be found in Remak (1967). Although most the authors in the volume edited by Evans and von Strandmann (1988) come to no definite conclusions, I admire their dispassionate tone, which stands in stark contrast to the narrowness or partisanship, both open and covert, of most of the standard studies. However, it is only fair to say that the chapter by von Strandmann is highly partisan in arguing the majority position: that Germany was most guilty of instigating the war.

Like all the other analyses of the origins of World War I published since 1977, von Strandmann did not cite the study by Goodspeed (1977), which plays a large part in my analysis. Of the studies published since 1984, von Strandmann was the only one to cite Kennan's (1984) study. Von Strandmann cited Kennan's study three times but very briefly. He criticized several specific points that Kennan made, especially his conclusion that the alliance between France and Russia made World War I inevitable. But von Strandmann's criticisms were weakly documented and ignored Kennan's overall thesis. This response to Kennan's powerful study was superficial, almost a formality.

Of course, there is no way of knowing why the two most powerful of the recent studies of the origins of World War I have been all but ignored. One possiblity is that they both go so much against the grain of the established position among experts that they have found it expedient to act as if these studies do not exist. If such is the case, it would not be the first time such a reaction has occurred in the history of scholarship.

A useful comparative study of the causes of war can be found in a book of great scope by Blainey (1988), a survey of the virtually innumerable wars fought between nations since 1700. Although descriptive and abstract, like Joll and most of the other better studies, the author deftly pointed out the utter uselessness of conventional wisdom about the causes of wars. Although he did not make the point explicitly, Blainey's analysis strongly suggested that we do not understand human behavior, either in the small or in the large. Like the causes of most human actions, the causes of war remain a mystery and an enigma.

Given the large number of prior studies on the origins of the war, and the diversity of their approaches to the problem, some comments on how the problem has been defined to this point are in order. Some of the earlier studies were purely descriptive or attempted to be. They ignored the problem of causation or at least did not deal with it explicitly. The way in which authors titled their studies usually revealed their overall approach. Descriptive studies used the phrase "the coming of World War I" (Schmitt, 1930; Laqueur and Moss, 1966; Evans and von Strandmann, 1988) or some similarly passive construction, such as "the approach of the First World War" (Bosworth, 1983; Berghahn, 1973) or "the outbreak of the First World War" (Lee, 1963). Kennan's (1984) study was an exception. Although he used a passive construction in his subtitle (the coming of the First World War), his study moved from description to generalization. Several studies had completely descriptive titles that involved, for example, only a date, such as *July, 1914*.

Another common approach was to explicitly discuss causation, but only briefly and in passing. For example, in what was otherwise a useful and balanced discussion, Sontag's (1933) approach to causation was to reject an analysis made by other authors. He acknowledged that Germany should share some of the blame for beginning the war but rejected the contention that Germany alone was responsible. However, he did not offer his own counterhypothesis. This kind of maneuver occurred in many of the studies.

The most common approach was to make a strong and explicit statement about causality but only about one country, usually Germany. The most notorious example is the work of Fischer (1967, 1975). One of the chief criticisms of his work is that he failed to compare the causal sequences he attributed to Germany with similar sequences in the other major participants (Koch, 1972; Moses, 1975). The contributions in this vein may not be completely erroneous, but they are certainly narrow and incomplete, neglecting the big picture in favor of the small.

Studies in this genre usually used a word or phrase in their titles that was stronger than the "outbreak" or "coming." Some of the title words in these studies were "causes," "roots," "genesis," and two words that imply causation, "culpability" and "guilt," as in Barnes (1928). The most commonly used word was "origins," as in Fay (1966), Albertini (1967), Lafore (1965), Fleming (1968), Turner (1970), Steiner (1977), Kieger (1983), Lieven (1983), Joll (1984), Hentig (1989), and Remak (1967). I single out Remak's study for criticism, not because of its weakness, but because of its strength. It comes closest to the kind of analysis I believe to be needed: an assessment of causation that is comparative rather than limited to a single country, person, or event.

Remak (1967, pp. 133–143) ranked the major participants in the following order in terms of the part they played in instigating the war: Austria, Serbia, Russia, Germany, England, and France. The eleven pages in which he explained his rankings, from the most culpable (Austria) to the least (France), formed a coherent narrative. But his explanation seemed arbitrary, if not chaotic. His reason for ranking Austria, Serbia, and Russia so high was that they all made overt moves toward war before the other three powers, either mobilization or a declaration of war or both. He ranked Germany, England, and France lower because they went to war only after the first three had done so.

Remak's explanation of the ranking of Germany, England, and France relative to each other shifted from the proximate issue of overt war moves to more distal issues. Germany was ranked fourth largely because for many years it had planned a highly detailed, aggressive move against France, through Belgium, the Schlieffen plan. England was ranked next because of its imperialism and control of the seas for the hundred years prior to the war. France was least culpable, in Remak's view, because it was attacked and did not have aggressive war plans, as did Germany, or a large number of colonies and control of the seas, as England did.

Although Remak's analysis was thoughtful, its piecemeal nature raised a host of questions. With respect to the high ranking given to Germany, many of Fischer's critics have pointed out that there is a vast difference between having war plans and instigating war. Remak chose to ignore the more proximate question of comparing each country's response to the crisis moment by moment. The same criticism applies to his explanation of England's rank; Remak neglected to tell us the causal links whereby imperialism and control of the seas led to war.

Finally, perhaps the most glaring difficulty in Remak's analysis was his ranking of France as the least responsible for the onset of the war. His explanation, that France was attacked by Germany, referred only to the highly visible surface of conflict without taking into account the underlying realities. He acknowledged that France conspired with Russia against Germany and Austria but did not seem to give this fact the same weight as the overt attack by Germany. Remak, like all the other researchers who have sought to understand the origins of the war, faced the difficult problem of selecting and comparing the motives and actions of a large number of individuals and groups in an extremely complex situation.

Remak's ranking of Austria, Serbia, and Russia high in culpability implied a neglect of the covert springs of behavior in favor of the overt. In particular, it ignored or discounted the possibility of conspiracy as a a key factor in causation of collective events. French diplomacy may have played a considerable role in the genesis of the war; in particular, the evidence suggests that French diplomacy led to a conspiracy with Russia and Serbia. This conspiracy seems to have led to the assassination of the archduke and, in the preemptive mobilization by Russia, two key events in the chain that led to war. In the absence of a theory, it is tempting to point only to the most obvious element in a situation, simplifying it by using only commonsense concepts.

Theory and Methods

It seems to me that the arbitrariness and confusion to be found in the explanations of this particular problem grow out of a more general problem in the human studies: the lack of explicit models of causation of any kind of behavior. In the absence of a commonly accepted model, each author is left with the unenviable task of creating his or her own model. I believe that this is the main reason that so little progress has been made in understanding the origins of World War I and other wars. (I will return to this issue at the end of this book.)

In this context, my reassessment of Stoessinger's (1990) study is both appreciative and critical. I accept his analysis of the parts played by Austria-Hungary and by Germany in the immediate triggering of the war. This part of his analysis was masterful. But I extend it by adding the roles played by France, Russia, and England. His portrayal of them as victims of the aggression by the Central Powers seems to me erroneous. On the contrary, all played more or less equal roles in causing the war. To persist in locating causation in one or the other nation may signal that the scholar has become almost as emotionally enmeshed in the conflict as the participants. Whatever the tone of voice or content, it is difficult to avoid blaming, or whitewashing, if one nation is singled out for analysis.

For his assessment of the causes of World War I, Stoessinger analyzed three exchanges that occurred immediately prior to the outbreak of hostilities. The first was between the kaiser and Franz Joseph, the emperor of Austria-Hungary, Germany's ally (pp. 3–5). The second was the "Willy-Nicky" telegrams (pp. 11–14). Willy was Kaiser Wilhelm of Germany, and Nicky was Czar Nicholas of Russia (they were first cousins). The third is two notes from Lord Grey, prime minister of England, to the kaiser and the kaiser's private responses to them (pp. 13–14).

Stoessinger's analysis focused on the kaiser's reactions since he was the recipient of all three sets of communications. Stoessinger said nothing about the communications given and received by France, thus entirely omitting one of the principal parties. I argue that Stoessinger's method of selection of texts led him to erroneous conclusions. His analysis was doomed from the outset since it began by excluding one of the parts of the system, France, rather than considering all of them.

Stoessinger was not alone among analysts in excluding France from consideration, although few of them did so completely. A more representative method was to downgrade France's role by making it subsidiary to that of some other nation. An example is provided by Williamson's (1988) analysis, which discussed France only insofar as it was an ally to Russia. Williamson's discussion began on a tendentious note: "World War I began in eastern Europe. The war started when Serbia, Austria-Hungary, Russia and Germany decided that war or the risk of war was an acceptable policy option"(p. 225).

The implication of these two sentences, which exclude France from consideration, is that wars can be started only by nations whose boundaries are contiguous to the location of the earliest declaration of war, i.e., Austria-Hungary and Serbia, surely a flagrant non sequitur. By this kind of reasoning, since Chile is in South America, then the United States could have had nothing to do with the destabilization of the Allende government. Nevertheless, the subsequent discussion brought in French activities as if they were subservient to those of Russia. Like Stoessinger's, Williamson's conclusions seemed to be determined by his initial assumptions. I argue, however, that to resolve this problem, all the nations, the parts, and the system in which they were involved must be considered.

Family systems theory (Bowen, 1978) suggests that in cases of interminable conflict, all parties are more or less equally involved in causing the conflict. The same theory also suggests that it is impossible to point to a single event as causal; in interminable conflict, each event is part of a long causal chain.

Outbreak of World War I

On June 28, 1914, the archduke of Austria and his wife were assassinated during a visit to Sarajevo. On July 5, the kaiser pledged Germany's "faithful support" to Austria for punitive action against Serbia. As Stoessinger (1990) pointed out, Wilhelm used a special term in his declaration of support, promising to be *Nibelungentreue*. The Nibelung is a blood bond from Teutonic legend that is sacred and irrevocable. The kaiser was deeply attached to Archduke Ferdinand and his wife. When the kaiser heard of their assassination, he reacted emotionally, pledging himself to support Austria whatever the consequences. This was an utterly reckless act since it amounted to giving Austria a blank check. This act represented Germany's hand on the final trigger.

Austria-Hungary had been hesitating about responding to the assassination because Berchtold, the foreign minister, was unsure of German support. But when the kaiser sent Berchtold a blank check, he issued an ultimatum to Serbia that contained a series of conditions arrogant and insulting enough to ensure noncompliance. The phrasing of this ultimatum, calculated to insult, was Austria's contribution to the actual starting of the war. When Serbia failed to comply to the letter, Austria declared war on Serbia. (I will return to the Austrian ultimatim in Chapter 6 when I consider a hypothetical solution to the crisis of July 1914.)

When the kaiser learned of the Austrian declaration of war against Serbia, he sent a conciliatory note to his cousin, the czar of Russia, offering to act as a mediator and to hold back Austria from fighting until a peaceful settlement could be reached:

> It is with the gravest concern that I hear of the impression which the action of Austria against Serbia is creating in your country. ... With regard to the hearty and tender friendship which binds us both from long ago with firm ties, I am exerting my utmost influence to induce the Austrians to deal straightly to arrive at a satisfactory understanding with you. I confidently hope you will help me in my efforts to smooth over difficulties that may still arise.
>
> Your very sincere and devoted friend and cousin. (Stoessinger, 1990, p. 12)

At virtually the same moment, Nicholas had also sent a note to the kaiser:

> Am glad you are back. In this most serious moment, I appeal to you to help me. An ignoble war has been declared on a weak country. The indignation in Russia shared

fully be me is enormous. I foresee that very soon I shall be overwhelmed by the pressure brought upon me and be forced to take extreme measures which will lead to war. To try and avoid such a calamity as a European war, I beg you in the name of our old friendship to do what you can to stop your allies from going too far. (Stoessinger, 1990, p. 13)

The telegrams appear to suggest that both monarchs wanted to avoid war.

Wilhelm responded to the czar's telegram by wiring his cousin not to take military measures, i.e., mobilization, that Austria would interpret to be threatening. The czar answered on July 30, "Thank you heartily for your quick answer. The military measures which have now come into force were decided five days ago for reasons of defense on account of Austria's preparations. I hope from all my heart that these measures won't in any way interfere with your part as mediator which I greatly value. We need your strong pressure on Austria to come to an understanding with us" (Stoessinger, 1990, p. 13). The tone of kaiser's response abruptly changed when he received this note. His comments on the margin of the telegram have been preserved: "According to this the Czar has simply been tricking us with his appeal for assistance and has deceived us. ... Then I must mobilize too. ... The hope that I would not let his mobilization measures disturb me in my role of mediator is childish, and solely intended to lure us into the mire. ... I regard my mediation action as brought to an end" (Stoessinger, 1990, p. 13). Instead of responding to the czar's continuing support for conciliation, the Kaiser reacted to a detail in the second sentence that he had apparently not known before: that Russia had made the decision for mobilization five days earlier.

The second exchange also involved the kaiser's reaction to a telegram, this time from Lord Grey, who warned on July 30, "If war breaks out, it [would] be the greatest catastrophe that the world has ever seen." The kaiser's reaction was again highly emotional, as his note on the telegram suggested: "This means they will attack us; Aha! The common cheat." On one of Grey's later notes, the kaiser wrote: "The net has been suddenly thrown over our head, and England sneeringly reaps the most brilliant success of her persistently prosecuted, purely anti-German world policy, against which we have proved ourselves helpless, while she twists the noose of our political and economic destruction out of our fidelity to Austria, as we squirm isolated in the net" (Stoessinger, 1990, p. 14).

Stoessinger gave a name to the emotional quality of the kaiser's reactions to Grey's notes; he called it "paranoia" (p. 13), an interpretation I challenge. Stoessinger also interpreted the notes from Grey and from the czar to be entirely in good faith, which I also challenge. After receiving the notes from the czar and from Grey, the kaiser issued an ultimatum to the Russians to immediately demobilize. When they refused, he ordered full mobilization for Germany. Since Russia had already begun full mobilization, the two movements together meant war. These telegrams and notes and the kaiser's reactions to them constitute the basic data for this chapter. The rest of what follows is my interpretation of the context and the meaning of these texts.

One purpose of my analysis is to challenge and modify Stoessinger's interpretation of these communications. Before beginning, I wish to describe the larger study of which his comments on the onset of World War I are a part. Stoessinger compared the beginnings of six other sets of wars in addition to World War I: Hitler's attack on Russia, the U.S. wars in Korea and Vietnam, the wars between India and Pakistan, those between Israel and the Arabs, and the Iran-Iraq war. By comparing the onset of these wars, he came to several conclusions about the causes of war.

His first conclusion (p. 209; emphasis added) concerned the role of leaders of nations as compared to impersonal forces:

> I am less impressed by the role of abstract forces, such as nationalism, militarism, or alliance systems, which traditionally have been regarded as the causes of war. Nor does a single one of the seven cases indicate that economic factors played a vital part in precipitating war. The personalities of leaders, on the other hand, have often been decisive. The outbreak of World War I illustrates this point quite clearly. Conventional wisdom has blamed the alliance system for the spread of the war. Specifically, the argument runs, Kaiser Wilhelm's alliance with Austria dragged Germany into the war against the Allied Powers. This analysis, however, totally ignores the role of the Kaiser's personality during the gathering crisis. Suppose Wilhelm had had the fortitude to continue his role as mediator and restrain Austria instead of engaging in *paranoid delusions* and accusing England of conspiring against Germany. The disaster might have been averted; the conventional wisdom would then have praised the alliance system for saving the peace instead of blaming it for causing the war. In truth the *emotional balance or lack of balance* of the German Kaiser turned out to be absolutely crucial.

I consider this conclusion vague and misleading. My interpretation is that the personalities of leaders had less to do with causing the war than did the system of relationships and communication tactics in which the leaders were involved. They were but parts of a more complex whole: the civilization in which they and their nations functioned.

Stoessinger's second conclusion (p. 210) concerned the role of the leaders' misperceptions. He argued that these wars were caused by leaders' mistaken perceptions about themselves, their allies, and their adversaries. They had what Stoessinger called "delusions" about their own strength and virtue, and those of their allies, and about the enemy's weakness and deceit. They also believed that a war was inevitable, which was in itself a powerful cause of war (p. 211).

Both the kaiser and Franz Joseph had nothing but contempt for the fighting prowess of the Russians, which turned out to be a grave error. Stoessinger provided many examples of such misperceptions and delusions on both sides in each of his seven cases. My analysis supports, extends, and conceptually organizes Stoessinger's interpretation. Misperception of self and others is a facet of bimodal alienation in a social system: alienation within (engulfment) and between (isolation) disputing groups.

My critique of his study focuses on three interrelated issues. First, Stoessinger's approach was *atheoretical.* His interpretations and findings were couched in the commonsense terms of ordinary language rather than deriving from concepts and propositions generated by a theory. (The second and third problems follow from his lack of theory.) Second, although he was dealing with a social system, his concepts and findings were *individualistic;* they concerned leaders and their personalities rather than the relationships between the leaders and their communication tactics. Third, his data were *incomplete.* He left out France from his analysis. If exchanges between France and Russia, and between France and England are included, a different picture emerges with respect to what Stoessinger called the Kaiser's "paranoia."

As already indicated, my analysis draws upon family systems theory, as stated by Bowen (1978). This theory concerns communication tactics between and within parties to a conflict. To understand the role of intentional secrecy and deception, Bowen's conception of triangling is crucially important. He noted that in what he called "dysfunctional families," two parties to a dispute seldom negotiate directly with each other with regard to the dispute (*leveling,* Satir, 1972). Rather, one party, A, conspires in secret with another party, C, against B, thereby excluding B instead of negotiating with B directly.

Triangling was a predominant pattern of French diplomacy in the years preceding World War I, with France extremely active in conspiring with Russia and with England against the Central Powers. The same pattern can also be seen within and between nations, with French leaders communicating secretly with English leaders but excluding their own countries.

One of the corollaries of family systems theory is that in dysfunctional families, it is usually a mistake to isolate a single member as the culprit. In interminable conflicts not only is there no single event that is a cause: there is also no single member to blame. All are caught up in a dysfunctional *system* of conflict. Blaming one party to an interminable conflict serves two functions: It ignores the systemic nature of the conflict and thereby denies the social nature of the human condition; and it serves to perpetuate the conflict. The one assigning blame becomes as emotionally enmeshed as the parties themselves, which destroys objectivity and impartiality.

Goodspeed's Study

Although the majority of historians still single out Germany has the prime instigator of the war, a countercurrent points to France as equally culpable. The clearest and most detailed statement of this point of view is by the Canadian historian Goodspeed (1977). Since his argument bears directly on the context of the discourse I am interpreting, I give a brief summary of his position.

Goodspeed (1977, pp. viii, chapters 1–5) argued that of all the major powers, France was the most powerfully motivated to start a war. He proposed that France experienced its defeat in the Franco-Prussian War (1871) as a humiliation, one that continued to rankle because of the loss of the provinces of Alsace and Lorraine. He argued that the French government's policies during the years from 1871 to 1914 were strongly influenced by the motive of revanche (revenge). This motive was seldom publicly avowed, as suggested by Gambetta's advice to the French about the defeat of 1871: "Speak of it never; think of it always," a counsel of obsession, denial, and bypassing of shame (cited in Buthman, 1970, p. 20).

Goodspeed argued that the French of this period were obsessed with recovering their lost provinces. This obsession seemed to increase, rather than decrease, with the passage of time; the French feared that the population of Alsace-Lorraine was becoming Germanized as the young people learned that language, rather than French, in their schooling. To remove what the French considered a stain on their honor, after the Franco-Prussian war, France created a firm alliance with Russia, the Dual Entente, for mutual aid against Germany. Even though France was a republic and Russia an absolutist monarchy, France sought to help develop Russia into mighty military power as an ally in a defeat of Germany. In particular, France provided the loans that would enable Russia to build a railroad network so that its troops would have the mobility needed to help defeat the Central Powers.

Although French diplomatic policy toward Germany became aggressive immediately following the Franco-Prussian War, matters came to a head in 1912 with the rise to power of Poincaré as the French premier. His appointment was precipitated by the Agdir crisis, a quarrel between France and Germany over the French plan to acquire Morocco as a colony. France's wish to "annex" Morocco was foiled by Germany's resistance to the plan. The French public thought the premier, Caillaux, had been too submissive to the Germans. Poincaré, a native of Lorraine, was another matter entirely. He had said publicly that his generation "had no reason for existence other than the hope of recovering the lost provinces" (cited in Barnes, 1928, p. 25). When he came to power, French secret activity against Germany became much more intense and aggressive.

Two thrusts of this activity concern us here: the events leading to the assassination of Archduke Ferdinand (the immediate trigger of the war) and the attempts of the French to gain England as an ally in a possible war with Germany. Goodspeed argued that these two trains of events were intimately connected.

It is clear that England, unlike the other four major powers, attempted to remain neutral in the event of the war, at least at the level of public actions. France and Russia were pledged allies, as were Germany and Austria-Hungary. Both sets of allies sought repeatedly in the years leading up to war to assure themselves of England's position: The Dual Entente wanted assurance that England would enter the war; the Central Powers, that it would not. Until the very day of mobilization, England never gave a clear answer to either question. The leadership actually equivocated: Although allowing Germany to expect that England would remain neutral, it planned for military participation with the French.

Goodspeed argued that England's refusal to make a clear pledge to either side was one of the proximate causes of the war (p. 131). If the Central Powers had known that England would fight on the side of the Entente, the kaiser might have been less careless about pledging his support for whatever action Austria-Hungary decided to take toward Serbia. The kaiser was certain that the Central Powers could defeat the Entente if it was not aided by England, but he had doubts about defeating the three powers together. Similarly, France's leaders were convinced that the Entente would win with the aid of England but were anxious about winning without it.

Because of these two conjectures by French leadership, capturing England as an ally became the principal thrust of French diplomacy. Although not able to secure a formal treaty, the French gained a secret alliance because the English leadership was a house divided. Although a majority of the cabinet and of the public would never pledge involvement in a war on the Continent, a minority of the leadership, Grey, Asquith, Churchill, and others, did. They were able to do so because Grey was the foreign minister and because he was willing to act in secret.

Beginning in 1905, Grey arranged for secret meetings between the French and English General Staffs to plan for cooperation in the event of a war. He kept these meetings secret not only from the Central Powers but also from his own cabinet. By the time Poincaré came to power, England's involvement in a war was virtually a fait accompli. Grey and Poincaré triangled not only against Germany but also against England.

Less than a year after taking office, Poincaré took care to secure an opinion from the French General Staff as to the probable outcome of a war, should it occur during his premiership. He was told that the advantage would be on the side of France, assuming that Russia and England were its allies. It would appear that from the moment he secured this favorable opinion, all his considerable energy and skill were devoted to triggering a war.

Poincaré's problem was to instigate war in a way that assured the entry of Russia and England on the side of France. He probably assumed that if the French began a war by marching on Alsace and Lorraine, neither Russia nor England would involve itself. He may have decided that the ideal trigger would have its location in the Balkans and that its ostensible cause would be an action by one of the Central Powers. That is, the location in the Balkans would ensure Russian entry into the war, and the aggressive action by a Central Power would guarantee English entry.

Goodspeed traced the incredibly intricate plotting by the French that led to the assassination of the archduke. It is so byzantine that I give only the briefest summary here. Poincaré conspired with the prowar group in the Russian government to encourage nationalism in the Balkans against the domination of Austria-Hungary, particularly Serbian nationalism. Russia's motive was to reassert its dominance in that area against both Austria and Turkey.

In particular, Poincaré guaranteed that France would support Russia and the Balkan nations against Austria-Hungary, even if this meant war with the Central

Powers. French guarantees were essential in this matter since without them, neither Russia nor Serbia would have acted. That is, Russia would not have taken on Austria-Hungary alone because of the likelihood that Germany would also have been involved. For any of the Balkan nations, action without Russian guarantees would simply have meant annexation by Austria-Hungary.

Under these conditions, Russian diplomats constructed a plot with the most violent and irresponsible of the Balkan governments, Serbia, to assassinate the archduke. The actual assassins were members of a secret terrorist group, but as Goodspeed showed, this group was led by the highest officials of the Serbian government and coached by Russian military advisers. These details became known only in 1925, however (pp. 114–118).

We can use the concept of *interlocking triangles* to describe the web of deception that led to the assassination. Instead of negotiating directly with Germany about the dispute, France triangled with Russia, which triangled with Serbia, which triangled with the terrorist group. These three interlocking triangles excluded the three parties whose interests were connected with the outcome: Germany, Austria-Hungary, and England. It is possible that not even Lord Grey, who conspired with the French about military cooperation against the Germans, had knowledge of the assassination plot, much less the English antiwar majority. England was as much a target of the conspiracy as the Central Powers were.

Analysis of Lethal Discourse

Given knowledge of these interlocking triangles, the kaiser's emotional reaction to the czar's and Grey's notes takes on a new meaning. I consider his reactions to Grey's notes first since the backdrop of Germany's attempts to get assurances of England's neutrality casts the matter in a new light. England had refused to pledge its neutrality but also would not promise to enter the war on the side of France and Russia. In this context, Grey's warning about a war being "the greatest catastrophe the world has ever seen" can be read as the first indication of England's commitment to fight. To clarify this point, I consider some details in German strategic thinking.

According to Germany's war plans, France and Russia alone could be readily defeated, even though waging a war on two fronts against a much larger combined army would seem disadvantageous to Germany. The Russian army, even though much larger than the German army, was also more ponderous because of a lack of railway and other transportation. The German plan was to attack France first, safely ignoring the slow-to-mobilize Russian army. After quickly defeating the French by a massive thrust through Belgium, the entire German army could be brought to bear on defeating Russia.

The kaiser guessed, however, that the likelihood of a quick victory depended on England not entering the war. If an English army landed in France to help defend Paris, a quick victory became problematic. The actual events in the first month of the war confirmed the accuracy of this idea. Russia was slow to mobilize, as expected. Had it not been for the presence of the British army and the stiff resistance of the Belgians, Paris would probably have fallen with the German attack and with it the whole nation.

The implication of Grey's telegram was that England would enter the war on the side of France since a war of the Central Powers against France and Russia would be unlikely to last long and therefore would not be the catastrophe that Grey had predicted. It is important to realize that Lord Grey would have made exactly the same calculations. In his memoirs he reported that he and his clique decided for war because they did not want France to fall under German domination, which they thought would happen if France and Russia fought against the Central Powers alone.

For these reasons, Grey's telegram implied the very encirclement that the kaiser complained about in his private response. Even if the kaiser had been unaware of the joint war planning by the French and English General Staffs, the chain of reasoning just discussed implied it. The kaiser's emotional reaction was not paranoid, as Stoessinger's argued, but closer to being a sudden awakening to the realities around him.

The kaiser's reaction to the czar's admission that mobilization had been decided five days earlier (July 25) can also be interpreted in a new light. It would suggest to the kaiser that Russian mobilization had been planned prior to the Austrian declaration of war on Serbia on July 28. That is to say, although the Austrian mobilization was only partial, aimed at Serbia, full mobilization by the Russians could only be aimed at the Central Powers, implying collusion between France and Russia at the very least and perhaps England as well.

Since Russia had by far the largest army, its mobilization had to be the signal for mobilization by all the other powers, so that it was virtually a declaration of war. Had Russian mobilization been partial and subsequent to Austria's, it would have signaled only defense. But since it was complete and prior to Austria's move, it was a clear signal of offensive purpose and preplanning.

Taken out of this complex and extended context, the kaiser's highly emotional reaction to the two sets of notes can easily be seen as violent overreactions (as in Stoessinger's [1990, p. 13] view that the second note from the czar "completely destroyed [the Kaiser's] sense of balance." However, in context, his reactions seem the normal response of one who justifiably felt betrayed.

A closer comparison of the contents of the czar's telegrams as against the kaiser's provides further support for Goodspeed's interpretation. In this comparison, I draw upon the description of dysfunctional communication tactics found in family system theory (Bowen, 1978). I show how microscopic analysis of texts support an argument at the macrolevel.

In the czar's first note, there are several indications of indirection, denial of responsibility, and threat. There is a slight indirection in the fourth sentence: "The indignation in Russia shared fully by me is enormous." A more direct acknowledgment of responsibility would have been a sentence such as *"I am indignant, as are my subjects."

The choice of the word *indignation* particularly suggests self-righteous anger and therefore, perhaps, rather than anger alone, shame-anger, with the shame component unacknowledged. This sentence is also used to prepare for the intense denial of responsibility and threat in the next sentence: "I foresee that very soon I shall be overwhelmed by the pressure brought upon me and be forced to take extreme measures which will lead to war."

Although phrased in polite language, the czar's note actually threatens war and at the same time denies his responsibility for it and even the responsibility of Russians; it is not his fault or theirs, but Austria's. The czar seems to see the coming war as exterior and constraining, with himself and his compatriots playing no part in its causation. By comparison with the czar's note, the kaiser's is a monument to directness, acknowledgment of responsibility, and absence of threat. He simply offers his services as mediator and says that he will restrain the Austrians.

The czar's second note continues in the same vein as his first. The second sentence contains a denial of his responsibility for his own actions, as did the first: "The military measures which have now come into force were decided five days ago for reasons of defense on account of Austria's preparations." It is Austria that is to blame for his actions, not himself.

Note also the awkward syntax in the two occurrences of the passive voice in this sentence; he does not say, *"I have decided to mobilize the army," which would have been direct and forceful. The indirection, vagueness, and denial of personal responsibility in this sentence strongly suggest either deception, self-deception, or both. Did the czar have a guilty conscience, was he trying to deceive his cousin, or was he doing both?

In any case, both of the czar's telegrams strongly suggest bimodal alienation. The threat implied in the telegrams, and the blaming of Austria, suggest isolation from without against both Germany and Austria. The vagueness, passive tenses, and indirection all suggest that the czar is fooling himself by denying his own feelings and responsibility for the threats he is making. In engulfed relations, one gives up parts of oneself to be loyal to one's group. The giving up of parts of self corresponds to what Melvin Seeman (1975) called "self-estrangement" in his analysis of alienation.

I now return to the historical record for collateral evidence that is relevant to my interpretation of these texts. The issue of the early mobilization of the Russian army brings us to the most bizarre episode that Goodspeed and others unearthed in the events leading to the war, the meeting of Poincaré and his entourage with the czar in St. Petersburg on July 15th–18th. This meeting occurred immediately following the assassination of the archduke and just before the czar's decision to mobilize.

The trip of the French premier to meet the head of a foreign state would have been unusual enough whatever the circumstances. But in this case, since it took place when the peace of Europe was at stake (because of the assassination), the eyes of the world were upon it. What transpired during the three-day meeting? The answer is, no one knows. There was no announcement of the outcome at the time or afterwards by participants from either side. What is extraordinary is that the mystery has never been removed since none of the participants clarified the matter, not even in their memoirs. Comments in the memoirs were brief, bland, and vague. Whatever occurred has been obliterated from history.

In the face of such an absence of information, Goodspeed examined the circumstantial evidence that would link the meeting to the onset of the war. He argued that since convictions in courts of law can be made upon the basis of circumstantial evidence alone, scholars should not hesitate to make similar judgments since the stakes in a case like this are so much higher. Goodspeed proposed that the evidence all points to collusion between the French and the Russians to instigate the war. In effect, Poincaré and the czar could have decided that the Russians would mobilize before the Austrians. From the French point of view, such a premature action would have a triple advantage: It would ensure a war, it would ensure Russian entry into the war, and it would provide a military advantage to the French. That is, the quicker Russian mobilization, the sooner German troops would be needed on the Russian front, removing them from an attack on France.

It may be significant that the official French diplomatic history of the war went to the extraordinary length of stating that the Austrian general mobilization occurred first and used forged documents to support the claim. It is also significant that all the participants sought to put their own actions in the best light but only the French and the Russians used forged documents in their official histories (Goodspeed, 1977, p. 137). Secrecy and deceit appear to have been instrumental not only in the causing the war but also in continuing the interminable conflict from which it grew.

A Family Quarrel

In the light of this discussion, Simmel's support for the social functions of secrecy (and, more recently, Komarovsky [1967]) seems ill-founded. This position, for which there is little actual evidence, is on the verge of becoming another article of faith in modern social science. For further evidence that seems to contradict Simmel, see Cottle (1980), who suggested that children's shameful secrets have disastrous effects, and Retzinger (1991), who showed how deception and secrecy produce alienation in marriages (see Chapter 1).

The broadest critique of secrecy was by Bok (1983). Although her analysis was comprehensive and precisely balanced, her conclusions were overwhelmingly opposed to secrecy in public matters, except under highly delimited circumstances. My analysis supports and extends hers by adding the component of self-deception: Secrecy, deception, and self-deception support and feed into one another, generating and reflecting alienation between and within persons and nations. Far from being functional, as Simmel claimed, secrecy and deception seem to be generated and supported by the status quo, the social arrangements that distribute power, wealth and esteem.

Following the lead of family systems theory, we can look at the major wars of the last hundred years as an interminable conflict in the family of nations. My analysis of origins of the World War I points in this direction. All five of the large nations that began it were equally involved. In the long term, the militarism of Germany and France and the secret diplomacy of France were certainly factors. In the period immediately preceding hostilities, the kaiser's blank check to Austria, and the active instigation of war against Serbia by Austria-Hungary and by France and Russia against Germany were equally important.

A systems analysis suggests that the listing of factors, however detailed and accurate, is not a parsimonious explanation. In family systems, conflicts of long duration and limitless destructiveness are caused, not by individual parties or specific events, but by the elemental structure/process of the social system in which they occur. Since 1870, nations in the world system have been trapped in bimodal alienation. War fever, the lust for conflict whatever the cost, can occur because members of the public within each nation maintain a false solidarity (engulfment) with one another and fail to identify with the enemy as persons like themselves (isolation).

My emphasis on the importance of deception and self-deception in understanding social systems is also found in O'Connor (1987, pp. 182–183): "Theory is no more or less than the critique of the self-deceptions which we use to legitimate to ourselves the deceptions of others. This means simply that we cannot know why we are deceived or why we deceive others until we first know why others deceive themselves and why we deceive ourselves. No trust, hence no morality, is possible without knowledge of our own and others' self-deceptions."

It might be argued that by concentrating entirely on alienation, my analysis has concerned only subjective causes, neglecting the "objective" causes of wars, such as scarcity of resources and cultural and linguistic differences. However, I counter by proposing that objective differences can always be negotiated where there is free communication and an absence of unacknowledged emotions. That is, however great the conflict of interests, there will always be some most rewarding or perhaps least punishing compromise.

In some ways the arguments that favor objective causes are another form of denial and projection: It is not we humans who make war, but objective conditions. If not tempered by part/whole understanding, structural explanations of human actions inadvertently become part of the causal chain that leads to war.

The realist interpretations of conflict insist that material conditions, money, territory, and technology play a part in causing war, which, of course, they do. But these same interpetations also insist, sub voce, that only material conditions are causal, surely a non sequitur. Such an argument seems blind to the force of human motives, perceptions, and emotional responses to material conditions. It represents an a priori assumption that of the two parts of human action, stimulus and response, only the stimulus is causal.

Family systems theorists have pointed out how unending conflict is generated in families when members focus only on topics, such as money, sex, and children, while ignoring relationships and feelings. If members are disrespectful in their manner, they insult each other continually. In this way any topic can become the cause of conflict. The obverse is that if members are respectful in their manner, any conflict can be resolved or at least reduced to manageable levels. The realists' arguments about material conditions are parallel to the focus on topics in family systems. To paraphrase Shakespeare's character Hotspur (*Henry the Fourth*), anything can become a cause for fighting when honor is at stake.

To this point, my analysis has concentrated on the actions of leaders of nations, with little attention to the masses of people within these nations. A true systems theory, however, implies that the peoples of these nations are just as much a part of the chain of causation as their leaders. This postulate gains support from the work of Ecksteins (1989, pp. 56–64), who described the crowds in Berlin, St. Petersburg, Vienna, Paris, and London.

In Berlin and the other major cities in Germany, large crowds began to form on Saturday, July 25, awaiting Serbia's answer to the Austrian ultimatum. Beginning on Thursday, July 30, excited crowds filled the streets of Berlin, remaining "an almost permanent feature of the German capital for the next seven crucial days" (p. 58). Both in arriving and leaving their sessions in the capital, the kaiser and his advisers had difficulty getting through the throng on the Unter den Linden on the next day. "All the major decision makers are confronted directly by the massive outpouring of enthusiasm from the Berlin public. None of them has ever witnessed such demonstrations before. None of them can ignore the popular mood" (pp. 59–60). By August 1, the crowd had grown to a huge size, estimated at from one to three hundred thousand people (p. 60). The order for German mobilization was "made against the back drop of mass enthusiasm. No political leader could have resisted the popular pressures for decisive action" (p. 61). "Elsewhere in Germany, whether in Frankfurt, Munich, Breslau or Karlsruhe, the scenes are similar. ... Emotionally Germany has declared war by July 31 ... , certainly on Russia and France. Given the intensity of public feelings, it is inconceivable that the kaiser can, at this point, turn back" (p. 62).

Although Ecksteins did not make the point explicitly, he implied that similar mob scenes were occurring in all the other capitols. In the illustrations (following p. 174), he showed photographs of vast crowds in Berlin, Paris, St. Petersburg, and London. The crowd, he said, was as potent a force in causing the war as the leaders. A war fever swept though the participating nations, involving virtually everyone, as suggested by a systems theory approach.

Even the leading intellectuals were caught up. Freud and Weber, to mention only two of them, were both of the opinion that a war would be a cleansing experience. Of the few who had a clearer vision of the consequences of a war, the poet Yeats and the woman he loved, Gonne, stood out. Gonne's critique of the war, in a letter written by her (Gonne and Yeats, 1993) on August 26, 1914, was particularly prescient: "This war is an inconceivable madness which has taken hold of Europe—It is unlike any other war that has ever been. It has no great idea behind it. Even the leaders hardly know why they have entered into it, and certainly the people do not. ... The victors will be nearly as enfeebled as the vanquished." Unlike the leading politicians, intellectuals, and social scientists, Gonne was crystal clear on the two most important features of the war: that it would be the most destructive event in the history of the world and that there was no good reason for it. Her comment that the leaders and people did not know why they were going to war parallels my argument that the emotional and relational roots of the war were deeply repressed. I will return to this feature in Chapter 6 in discussing the idea of the "tensions" that are part of the causes of war.

I do not believe that Gonne had the gift of second sight, as she herself would have liked to believe. I think rather that her worldview as artist, Irish nationalist, feminist, and occultist distanced her from the collective illusion that held most of Europe in thrall.

Contemporary biography provides further hints at the causes of war fever. A representative instance occurs in the life of the philosopher Wittgenstein, a citizen of Austria at the beginning of the war. Wittgenstein's life was closely tied to that of Russell, his teacher, who was a close observer of World War I. One biographer (Monk, 1990, pp. 111–112; emphasis added) explained Wittgenstein's motives in the social context of the times:

> Although a patriot, Wittgenstein's motives for enlisting in the army were more complicated than a desire to defend his country. His sister Hermine thought it had to do with: "an intense desire to take something difficult upon himself and to do something other than purely intellectual work." It was linked to the desire he had felt so intensely since January, to "turn into a *different person.*"
>
> The metaphor he had then used to describe his emotional state serves equally to describe the feeling that pervaded Europe during the summer of 1914—the sense of perpetual seething, and the hope that "things will come to an eruption once and for all." Hence the scenes of joy and celebration that greeted the declaration of war in each of the belligerent nations. The whole world, it seems, shared Wittgenstein's madness of 1914. In his autobiography, Russell describes how, walking through the cheering crowds in Trafalgar Square, he was amazed to discover that "average men and women were delighted at the prospect of war." Even some of his best friends, such as George Trevelyan and Alfred North Whitehead, were caught up in the enthusiasm and became "savagely warlike."
>
> We should not imagine Wittgenstein greeting the news of war against Russia with unfettered delight, or succumbing to the hysterical xenophobia that gripped the European nations at this time. None the less, that he in some sense *welcomed* the war

seems indisputable, even though this was primarily for personal rather than nationalistic reasons. Like many of his generation (including, for example, some of his contemporaries at Cambridge, such as Rupert Brooke, Frank Bliss and Ferenc Békássy), Wittgenstein felt that the experience of facing death would, in some way or other, *improve* him. He went to war, one could say, not for the sake of his country, but for the sake of himself. In the diaries Wittgenstein kept during the war (the personal parts of which are written in a very simple code) there are signs that he wished for precisely this kind of consecration. "Now I have the chance to be a *decent human being*," he wrote on the occasion of his first glimpse of the enemy, "for I'm standing eye to eye with death." It was two years into the war before he was actually brought into the firing line, and his immediate thought was of the spiritual value it would bring. "Perhaps," he wrote, "the nearness of death will bring *light into life*. God enlighten me." What Wittgenstein wanted from the war, then, was a transformation of his whole personality, a "variety of religious experience" that would change his life irrevocably. In this sense, the war came for him just at the right time, at the moment when his desire to "turn into a different person" was stronger even than his desire to stay alive.

There are a number of points in this passage that are relevant here. Russell's comments about the support of crowds for the war, in this case the crowds in London, support those of Ecksteins. Elsewhere, Russell (1916) classified this war as one whose base source was vanity and prestige rather than conflicts of interest. This analysis, which was the reason he chose to be a conscientious objector, closely parallels my own since "prestige" is a codeword for honor and the avoidance of shame. Note also that this passage discussed four young men from three different countries, suggesting that all had the same basic motive for going to war: the hope that it would improve them (Brook and Bliss were English; Wittgenstein, Austrian; and Békássy, Hungarian). Although these men were on opposing sides (Austria-Hungary was an ally of Germany), they seem to have had the same motives, which were personal rather than political. These men may have wanted war because they were alienated from their respective societies. Because of their age and their education, they had yet to be integrated into positions of respect in their societies. Instead of investigating their feelings of alienation, they acted them out by going to war.

War and Social Science

It is understandable that nations and their leaders are lost in the nightmare of their own history, that they view the wars that they themselves create as exterior and constraining. Their own characters and social institutions were created by a dysfunctional civilization founded on secrecy, deceit, self-deception, and repressed emotion, the accompaniments of massive alienation.

Although alienation and shame are almost universally repressed at the level of governments in our civilization, repression may occur to different degrees. Shame appeared most deeply repressed in the stronger countries, England and Germany, and was therefore less obvious in their actions. That is, it could be seen most clearly at the level of character rather than at the level of institutions. Shame was close to surface in the actions and rationalizations of the weaker governments, France, Russia, and Austria-Hungary. I have already indicated how notions of honor, insult, and revenge played a major role in French politics during the period 1871–1914. Stoessinger (1990, pp. 6–7) pointed out comparable motives in the actions of the leaders of Austria-Hungary, with their denial of the weakness of their nation and their emphasis on maintaining their "prestige" among other nations in the face of their fading power.

To see the role of shame in English and German politics means focusing on the level of character. An approach to this problem can be found in the work of Hughes (1983), who compared the character of English and German leaders in the years prior to 1914. Her analysis of the German leadership in particular seems to support the approach I have taken here. Although she did not use the concept of shame, her data and interpretations suggested it.

Hughes suggested that the style of the German leaders was characterized by what she called "the fatalistic temper," the denial of one's own responsibility by projecting it onto the outer world. The best-known example of this maneuver was the reaction of German leaders to the initial stages of mobilization: "Events take control"(Fleming, 1968, p. 164). Rather than acknowledge that they themselves were contributing to events and that they had the power to interfere with them, these leaders projected this power onto "events."

The way in which the repression of shame led to the fatalistic temper was suggested by Hughes's (pp. 215–218) analysis of the character of the two male protagonists of a popular nineteenth-century German novel *Effie Briest*. One of the male characters in the novel receives what he experiences to be an insult from the actions of another man toward his wife, who is completely innocent. Even though he realizes the futility of dueling, he feels compelled to it because he has in a moment of "weakness" revealed his experience of insult to the other protagonist, his closest friend. Although Hughes did not name the shame component, it is clear from her description that the man who felt insulted is compelled to remove the stain from his honor because he anticipates seeing himself in a negative way in the eyes of the other man, the generic shame context. He acts out the code of honor to bypass shame.

Hughes's analysis of the character of the English leadership did not touch as clearly on the repression of shame as a motive. Perhaps unacknowledged shame was less of an issue, or it was more deeply repressed. More research may be needed on this issue. The repression of shame at the level of character probably did not influence English and German group behavior directly, the way it appears to have done in the cases of France and Austria-Hungary. Nevertheless, it still could have played a vital role since the English and German leaders missed the opportunity of interfering with the chain of events, even when they could clearly see their futility, somewhat like the protagonists in *Effie Briest*.

Perhaps the dysfunctional system between nations is invisible to national leaders and their publics because the same system occurs within their nations and within their own families, even their own characters. The triangling, threats and counterthreats, idealization of self and allies, vilification of enemies, and other tactics that led to World War I proceed apace in all nations and most families, wartime or peacetime, no matter. The war is everywhere (Suzanne Retzinger, personal communication). We have been down so long it looks like up. Unless this system is changed, it will continue to perpetuate itself until the end of time.

It may be that our job as social scientists is to at least awaken ourselves from this nightmare. How can one escape from the limitations of one's own character and social institutions? Although by no means an easy task, three directions might make a start. A first direction is that in studying a complex problem such as the one discussed here, one needs an explicit theory and method to help maintain one's objectivity in the face of the ocean of facts and the conflicting approaches. In this book I have called upon a theory generated from family systems approaches and the sociology of emotions. I have applied a method based on the analysis of discourse. This theory and this method have served as a guide through what might otherwise have been an overwhelming mass of studies and viewpoints.

Another theory and method that might bring some order to the study of the origins of wars are legal theory and practice. In courts of law there is already an existing framework for determining causation, a theory of human behavior and methods for presenting evidence as to actions and motives. In criminal law, for example, the prosecution must prove not only that the defendant committed a crime but also that he or she *intended* to do so. Conviction for a crime requires the presentation of physical and subjective evidence showing *mens rea*, criminal intent.

It is possible that the legal approach to proving conspiracy might solve some of the many problems of showing causation of collective actions and avoid some of the arbitrariness we have seen in explanations such as those by Remak (1967) and Williamson (1988). However, I am not saying that researchers need adopt all the features of the legal model; it seems particularly important that we ignore the issue of intent. In family and world systems, wars seemed less caused by human intentions than by alienation and the repression of emotions.

A second direction is the need for a new kind of understanding of self and society, what I have called "part/whole" understanding (Scheff, 1990). In this type of endeavor, one studies not only the part or the whole but also both together and the relationship between the two. In such an analysis, one escapes from entrapment in the situation being studied by commenting on it directly. In particular, one avoids singling out only one part or the other of the larger system for blame, the capitalists, the leaders, the men, the Germans. In Stoessinger's study of the origins of World War I, he included some detailed parts and some wholes, but he excluded others, notably the actions of France.

A good example of part/whole thinking can be found in the work of Elias (1978, 1982) on the civilizing process. He developed a theory of development of modernity, of our contemporary status quo, by considering verbatim texts, mostly advice manuals, literary works, and diplomatic notes, within the context of larger historical movements. In this way he was able to include the building of character, interpersonal relations, and the formation of national cultures and states within the same framework. His analysis was specialized, but it was also general, attempting to include many levels of analysis and disciplinary viewpoints. His work as a whole, like Goethe's before him, exemplified what I have called the "specialist-generalist" (Scheff, 1990; see also Mills's [1959] description of the sociological imagination).

To be sure, specialization of function is unavoidable in modern societies. Not everyone can be a brain surgeon. But we are under no compulsion to *think* in a specialized way. Hyperspecialization of both function and thinking may be no more than one of the myriad forms that alienation from others and from self takes in our civilization.

Of all the earlier approaches to the causes of World War I, the one that is closest to my own is that of Kennan (1984) in his study of what he called "the fateful alliance," the secret military treaty completed between France and Russia in 1894. There are many parallels between my theory, method, and findings and those of Kennan. The first involves methods. Like my study, Kennan used part/whole reasoning. The bulk of Kennan's book concerned his very close reading of verbatim letters and documents showing the origins of the treaty and the way in which it came to be written sequentially step by step.

Yet in his conclusion, Kennan proposed several extremely abstract generalizations about the causes of the war. Like my study, Kennan's fell in neither of the two camps; he did not evade the issue of causation, as those in the descriptive camp do, nor did he limit his conclusions to a single event, person, or nation, the approach in the other camp. Kennan used general concepts, but he was careful to ground them in concrete events, the essence of the part/whole approach.

Like my study, Kennan demurred from the majority position that Germany bore a heavier responsiblity for starting the war than the other powers. By giving so much prominence to the French-Russian alliance in the origins of the war, he implied that these two countries played as much a role as Germany or any other country did in instigating the war.

Finally, in his conclusions, Kennan seemed to imply a theory of alienation very much like the one proposed in this book. By comparing earlier wars with limited goals to World War I, in which total destruction of the enemy was the only goal, Kennan (p. 254) outlined a change from a mixture of solidarity and alienation between nations in the eighteenth and nineteenth centuries to one of virtually total alienation in the twenthieth:

> As late as the eighteenth century, wars, being conducted in the name of dynastic rulers rather than entire nations, were generally fought for specific limited purposes. The amount of force was made, if possible, commensurate to the purpose at hand—no more, no less. When the immediate objective had been obtained, or had proven

unobtainable, one desisted. One did not try to carry hostilities to the point of the total destruction of the adversary's armed power and his complete humiliation and political emasculation. For that, there was too keen an awareness of the ultimate community of fate of all dynasties.

Kennan went on to link the specialization of the professional establishment, especially the military establishment, nationalism, and alienation, to the causes of war: "Precisely because of the higher degree of specialization and professional concentration to which he was subject, the senior military figure of the new era tended to have his eyes riveted more exclusively on the technical-military aspects of his dedication than were those of his counterparts of earlier ages, and to be less familiar and less involved with the wider political interests military forces were supposed to serve."

In his discussion of nationalism, Kennan (pp. 256–257) focused on its emotional power in a way that parallels my analysis:

> The nation, as distinct from the dynastic ruler of earlier times, is—even in theory—a secular force. Ready as it is to invoke the blessing of the Almighty on its military ventures, it cannot claim the divine right of kings or recognize the moral limitations that right once implied. And it is outstandingly self-righteous—sometimes to the point of self-adoration and self-idealization—in its attitudes towards any country that appears to oppose its purposes or threaten its security. The kings and princes of earlier times were usually cynical, indeed; but their cynicism often related, in a disillusioned way, to themselves as well as to their rivals. The nation-state is cynical, too, sometimes pathologically so, but only in relation to opposing military-political force. In the view it takes of itself it is admiring to the point of narcissism. *Its* symbols always require the highest reverence; *its* cause deserves the highest sacrifice; *its* interests are sacrosanct. The symbols, causes, and interests of its international rivals are, by contrast, unworthy, disreputable, expendable. Once involved in a war, regardless of the specific circumstances that gave rise to the involvement in the first place, the nation-state fights for vague, emotional, essentially punitive purposes. *They,* the opponents, must be punished, made to regret their recalcitrance, made to be sorry. *We,* on the other hand, must be vindicated by victory; the justice of our cause must be confirmed (as though this proved something) by its very military triumph; *our* admirableness must be documented by *their* ultimate recognition of our superiority.

Kennan's (p. 257) last comment linked alienation, specialization, and nationalism in a way that closely parallels my proposal that bimodal alienation is the systemic cause of modern wars:

> These, as will readily be seen, are anything else but limited aims. And it is not difficult to see how beautifully they dovetail with the hopes and anxieties of military men charged with the planning or pursuing of sweeping military victories over hypothetical opponents in essentially purposeless wars. The nationalistic euphoria provides the moral-political justification for those visions of all-out military effort and of total military victory that unavoidably command the imagination, and shape the efforts, of the military planner. And between the two of them they tend to obliterate, in

minds of both statesmen and popular masses, all consciousness of that essential community of fate that links, in reality, all great nations of the modern world and renders the destruction of any one of them the ultimate destruction, too, of the country that destroyed it.

Although Kennan did not say so explictly, it is clear enough in context that his analysis of these generic causes applied equally to all the major participants in the war, not just to France and Russia. As in my conclusions, Kennan seems to argue for equal responsiblity among the participants. My statements are explict and somewhat flatfooted, Kennan's are more implicit and graceful, but we seem to reach a very similar conclusion linking war to alienation and emotion.

A third direction might lead to more self-understanding by social scientists. Our own understanding of social relationships is conditioned by those in our families, both our family of origin and our nuclear family. To some extent we have all learned to see the relationships in these two families as external and constraining, even though by the time we became teenagers, we were as active in sustaining them as anyone else. I propose that if social scientists are not to be as entrapped in social systems as everyone else, we must try to understand the relationships in our own families. With such understanding, and with the use of part/whole thinking, we then might help bring peace, not just between nations and not just during wartime.

The next chapter will continue the saga of what Goodspeed (1977) called "the German Wars," showing that the way in which World War I ended set up the conditions that led to World War II.

References

Albertini, L. 1967. *The Origins of the War of 1914*. London: Oxford Univ. Press.
Barnes, H. E. 1928. *In Quest of Truth and Justice*. Chicago: National Historical Society.
Berghahn, V. R. 1973. *Germany and the Approach of War in 1914*. New York: St. Martin's Press.
Blainey, G. 1988. *The Causes of War*. London: Macmillan.
Bok, S. 1983. *Secrets*. New York: Vintage Books.
Bosworth, R. 1983. *Italy and the Approach of the First World War*. New York: St. Martin's Press.
Bowen, M. 1978. *Family Therapy in Clinical Practice*. New York: Jason Aronson.
Buthman, W. 1990. *The Rise of Integral Nationalism in France*. New York: Octagon Books.
Cottle, T. 1980. *Children's Secrets*. New York: Anchor Books.
Durkheim, E. [1912] 1954. *The Elementary Forms of Religious Life*. New York: Free Press.
Ecksteins, M. 1989. *The Rites of Spring*. Boston: Houghton Mifflin.
Elias, N. 1972. *What Is Sociology?* London: Hutchison.
_____. 1978. *The History of Manners*. New York: Pantheon Books.
_____. 1982. *Power and Civility*. New York: Pantheon Books.
Evans, R. J., and H. P. von Strandmann. 1988. *The Coming of the First World War*. Oxford: Clarendon Press.

Fay, S. B. 1966. *The Origins of the World War*. New York: Free Press.

Ferguson, B. 1988. *The Anthropology of War*. New York: Occasional Paper of the Herman Guggenheim Foundation.

Fischer, F. 1967. *Germany's Aims in the First World War*. New York: Norton.

———. 1975. *War of Illusions: German Policies from 1911 to 1914*. New York: Norton.

Fleming, D. F. 1968. *The Origins and Legacies of World War I*. Garden City, NY: Doubleday.

Gaylin, W. 1984. *The Rage Within*. New York: Simon and Schuster.

Goffman, E. 1967. *Interaction Ritual*. Garden City, NY: Anchor Books.

Gonne, M., and W. B. Yeats. 1993. *The Gonne-Yeats Letters*. New York: Norton.

Goodspeed, D. J. 1977. *The German Wars: 1914–1915*. Boston: Houghton Mifflin.

Gottschalk, L., C. Winger, and G. Gleser. *Manual of Instruction for Using the Gottschalk-Gleser Content Analysis Scales*. Berkeley and Los Angeles: Univ. of California Press

Haas, J. 1990. *The Anthropology of War*. Cambridge: Cambridge Univ. Press.

Hentig, R. 1989. *The Origins of the First World War*. London: Routledge.

Hughes, J. 1983. *Emotion and High Politics*. Berkeley and Los Angeles: Univ. of California Press.

Jervis, R., N. Lebow, and J. Stein. 1985. *Psychology and Deterrence*. Baltimore: Johns Hopkins Univ. Press.

Joll, J. 1984. *The Origins of the First World War*. London: Longmans.

Kennan, G. 1979. *The Decline of Bismark's European Order*. Princeton: Princeton Univ. Press.

———. 1984. *The Fateful Alliance: France, Russia, and the Coming of the First World War*. New York: Pantheon Books.

Kieger, J. 1983. *France and the Origins of the First World War*. London: Macmillan.

Kissinger, H. 1957. *A World Restored: Metternich, Castlereigh, and the Problem of Peace, 1812–1822*. Boston: Houghton Mifflin.

Koch, H. W., ed. 1972. *The Origins of the First World War*. London: Macmillan.

Komarovsky, M. 1967. *Blue Collar Marriage*. Oxford: Oxford Univ. Press.

Laqueur, W., and G. Mosse, eds. 1966. *1914: The Coming of the First World War*. New York: Harper and Row.

Lafore, L. D. 1965. *The Long Fuse*. Philadelphia: Lippincott.

Lee, D. 1963. *The Outbreak of the First World War*. Boston: D. C. Heath.

Lewis, H. B. 1971. *Shame and Guilt in Neurosis*. New York: International Universities Press.

Lieven, D. C. 1983. *Russia and the Origins of the First World War*. London: Macmillan.

Lynd, H. 1958. *On Shame and the Search for Identity*. New York: Harcourt.

Macchiavelli, N. [1431] 1988. *The Prince*. New York: Cambridge Univ. Press.

Mills, C. W. 1959. *The Sociological Imagination*. Oxford: Oxford Univ. Press.

Monk, R. 1990. *The Duty of Genius*. New York: Free Press.

Moses, J. A. 1975. *The Politics of Illusion*. New York: Harper and Row.

O'Connor, J. 1987. *The Meaning of Crisis*. London: Basil Blackwell.

Peristiany, J. 1966. *Honor and Shame in Mediterranean Societies*. Chicago: Univ. of Chicago Press.

Remak, J. 1967. *The Origins of World War I*. New York: Holt, Rinehart and Winston.

Retzinger, S. M. 1991. *Violent Emotions: Shame and Rage in Marital Quarrels*. Newbury Park, CA: Sage.

Riches, D. 1986. *The Anthropology of Violence*. Oxford: Basil Blackwell.

Russel, B. 1916. *Justice in Wartime*. Chicago: Open Court.

Satir, V. 1972. *Peoplemaking*. Palo Alto, CA: Science and Behavior.

Scheff, T. J. 1990. *Microsociology: Discourse, Emotion, and Social Structure.* Chicago: Univ. of Chicago Press.

Scheff, T. J., and S. M. Retzinger. 1991. *Emotions and Violence: Shame and Rage in Destructive Conflicts.* Lexington, MA: Lexington Books.

Schmitt, B. E. 1930. *The Coming of the War, 1914.* New York: Scribner's.

Seeman, M. 1975. "Alienation Studies." *Annual Review of Sociology* 1:91–124.

Simmel, G. 1950. *The Sociology of Georg Simmel.* Glencoe, IL: Free Press.

Sontag, R. J. 1933. *European Diplomatic History.* New York: Appleton-Century.

Steiner, Z. 1977. *Britain and the Origins of the First World War.* London: Macmillan.

Stoessinger, J. 1990. *Why Nations Go to War.* London: St. Martin's Press.

Turner, L. C. 1970. *Origins of the First World War.* New York: Norton.

Turner, P., and D. Pitt. 1989. *The Anthropology of War and Peace.* Granby, MA: Bergin and Garvey.

Turney-High, H. H. 1949. *Primitive War.* Columbia: Univ. of South Carolina Press.

Williamson, S. 1988. "The Origins of World War I." In R. Rotberg , and T. Rabb (eds.) *The Origins and Preventions of Major Wars.* Cambridge: Cambridge Univ. Press.

5

The Origins of World War II: Hitler's Appeal to the Germans

Shame is a kind of anger turned in on itself. And if a whole nation were to feel ashamed it would be like a lion recoiling in order to spring.

—Karl Marx, *Early Writings*[1]

This chapter proposes a solution to the riddle of Hitler's appeal to the German masses. Following Lasswell (1960), I show how Hitler's psychopathology, his paranoia, and his continual humiliated fury produced a program responsive to the craving of his public for a sense of community and pride rather than alienation and shame. Since neither the alienation nor the shame was acknowledged, both Hitler and his public were trapped in a neverending cycle of humiliation, rage, and vengeful aggression. I describe the evidence for unacknowledged shame in Hitler's life and in his written statements (mainly *Mein Kampf*).

I propose that the alienation and shame-rage cycle in Germany was (and is) only part of a larger system of alienation and emotional repression within and between nations in the world social system. Hitler's rise to power was produced by the labeling, segregation, and stigmatization of Germany after its defeat in World

---

This chapter is based in large part on Chapter 8 of Scheff and Retzinger (1991). Used with permission of the publisher.

1. This statement is part of Marx's discussion of the beginnings of German nationalism in an 1843 letter to Ruge. Michael Billig called this passage to my attention.

War I. Unless the social and emotional features of the world system change toward more solidarity and less repression, unending warfare is the likely result.

The analysis in this chapter is not parallel to the discussion in the last chapter. There is no puzzle as to the causes of World War II: Everyone agrees that it was Germany's war from the beginning. If there is any puzzle, it is why the Allies waited so long to contest Hitler's blatant madness. That issue goes beyond the range of this book, having to do not only with physical exhaustion and depletion but also with a shame issue different from the one that is the main thread of my present argument, the shame-rage sequence. The ostrichlike stance of the Allies in the 1930s, particularly England, may be explained in part by shame-shame loops: being ashamed of being ashamed to the point of paralysis. This loop may underlie issues such as guilt and withdrawal as well as paralyzed indecision. Since there has been no adequate elucidation of the shame-shame sequence, the puzzle of Allied indecision awaits further work on the social psychology of emotion.

Earlier Studies

The problem in this chapter concerns another puzzle: the origins of Germany's challenge to the world in the 1930s. How could a fanatic like Hitler become the leader of a modern nation? Hitler's appeal to the German people has yet to be adequately explained. In his person, he was singularly unprepossessing, to say the least. From a logical point of view, his speeches were disasters; he rambled incoherently, with little order and less substance. His political program was no better; it was disorganized, vague, and silent on key issues.

Beneath the surface, matters were still worse. From the testimony of his intimates, Hitler's personality was bizarre to the point of madness. His delusions, phobias, sadism, sexual aberrations, and utter isolation are well documented. All the biographies clearly show manifold symptoms of severe mental illness.

The puzzle is that this extraordinarily unattractive madman had charismatic appeal not only to the masses but also to a large coterie of devoted followers. These individuals knew most or all of the unsavory details, yet were fanatically loyal. In this chapter I first review earlier attempts to resolve this problem. Building on these explanations, I outline a new approach that focuses on the emotional bases of charisma. I propose a new theory of the dynamics of shame that suggests that unconscious vengefulness motivated Hitler and connected him to his followers.

A conjecture by Lasswell (1960) provided the foundation for most discussion of Hitler's appeal. Lasswell proposed that successful leaders make assets out of their psychological difficulties by rationalization; they externalize their internal conflicts in political programs. Those whose personal needs exactly correspond to those of their countrymen and -women have charismatic, i.e., emotional, appeal.

Lasswell's proposal implied that if we are to understand Hitler's appeal during the years he came to power, we need to understand:

1. The personal needs of Germans in the mass;
2. Hitler's personality;
3. The linkage between Hitler and the German masses.

This is a problem of culture and personality, the link between the one and the many. Such problems were much discussed several decades ago but are now neglected. The central difficulty was the lack of a theory and a method for conceptualizing the link between individual and collective behavior. I use recent developments in theory and method for the study of emotions to provide such a link.

There are many studies of the first two listed issues, but the third, the link between Hitler and his public, is treated only briefly and casually. As a framework for discussion, I first summarize several approaches to the problem. Of the many discussions of the social bases of Hitler's rise to power, I review three representative ones: Mitchell (1983), Dahrendorf (1967), and Waite (1977). As in the case of most of the other studies, Mitchell's (1983) explanation of Hitler's appeal was quite brief (pp. 259–266) and very late in the text, the last eight pages. He proposed that a sequence of disasters lead to a state of anomie, the breakdown of an entire society (Germany's defeat in World War I, the humiliation of the Treaty of Versailles, the Great Inflation, and, finally, the Great Depression in 1929). These events created an economic, intellectual, political, and emotional crisis in Germany.

In this crisis, Hitler offered what seemed to many Germans attractive solutions. Of several concepts that Mitchell and others proposed, I emphasize two: anomie and shame. Instead of anomie, Hitler offered community (*Volksgemeinschaft*, "a community of the folk") and instead of humiliation, pride and self-confidence. The idea of the folkcommunity intimated a restoration of what had been lost: the traditional rural community from which many Germans had recently been wrenched. The community Hitler offered, "race and blood," seemed easily attainable by the masses; it was heedless of most of the usual distinctions (e.g., region, class, income, and education). It excluded only a small proportion of the population, mainly Communists and Jews.

Anomie, the breakdown of community and societal bonds, has been linked by most of the commentators to the rise of Hitler. Dahrendorf (1967) treated this issue in greatest detail. He suggested that anomie was prevalent in German society even before World War I because industrialization had come lately, rapidly, and more completely compared to England, the United States, and France. These latter countries had several hundred years to develop new forms of community during industrialization. Rapid, thorough industrialization led to a more extensive state of anomie in Germany than in the older industrial countries. Dahrendorf proposed that this condition provided the basis for the appeal of a totalitarian leader.

The other concept proposed by Mitchell (1983, p. 262) and others was that Hitler offered pride, instead of shame; a restoration of what Mitchell called "self-confidence"; and "an escape route from the deep pits of humiliation to nearly unlimited adventure." This same solution was implied in Mitchell's discussion of Hitler's ability to "direct popular emotions," although pride and shame were not named explicitly.

These same two dimensions of Hitler's appeal, restoring a lost sense of community and pride, were mentioned in virtually all other discussions, with about the same amount of detail as Mitchell, or less. In Waite's (1977) discussion, however, the issue of restoring lost pride was treated at greater length. He noted several times that Germans referred to the Treaty of Versailles as the "Treaty of Shame" and discussed the particular ways in which it triggered the crisis in the Weimar Republic. (Harry Steinhauer told me that after coming to power, Hitler usually referred to the Weimar Republic only as "fourteen years of shame and disgrace." In German this phrase carries much greater force than the English translation: *Vierzehn Jahren von Schmach und Schande!* It almost requires shouting to get it out, which is exactly what Hitler did. He used the phrase as an epithet.)

Germans felt betrayed; because of Wilson's Fourteen points, they expected a treaty of reconciliation. Instead the Treaty of Versailles transferred large parts of German territory to other nations, seized all German colonies, and excluded Germany from membership in the League of Nations as unworthy. The treaty spoke in general terms about disarmament, but in actuality only Germany was forced to disarm.

Apparently the most disturbing part of the treaty was one that involved a symbolic issue rather than material ones. In Article 231, Germany was required to confess sole responsibility for causing World War I, a patent absurdity. (I return to the issue of blame in my discussion of conflict in family and social systems.) Furthermore, the Germans were compelled to sign the treaty since they were threatened with continued blockade until they did. The blockade was in fact extended ten months beyond the end of the war, causing starvation and a further sense of injustice and betrayal.

As it turned out, the Allied treatment of Germany in the Treaty of Versailles was neither fish nor fowl: It visited suffering and humiliation without destroying the German capacity to make war. An earlier victor over the German tribes, Julius Caesar, had had a different policy: After defeating a tribe, he either killed every member or treated everyone generously because he feared revenge. Although the French feared revenge, the Allies neither scorched the German earth nor restored Germany to the community of nations. (For a treatment of the difference between reintegrative and isolating punishment, see Braithwaite, 1989.)

After recounting the realistic bases for the German sense of betrayal and humiliation, Waite went on to describe the irrational ones: the legend of the *Dolchstoss* (stab in the back) and the anti-Semitism to which it was closely tied. The stab-in-the-back legend was that the "November criminals," traitorous Jews and revolutionaries at home surrendered, rather than the victorious armed forces. This legend was pure fiction (Waite, 1977, p. 307). The military command compelled surrender well before the revolution; General Ludendorff forced an unwilling civilian government to sue for peace. Although both legends were false, Hitler always took them to be factual; they played an important role in his appeal.

Hitler's Personality

The need of Germans for solidarity and pride is prominent in a reverse way in the many studies of Hitler's psychopathology. They all stress Hitler's complete isolation from other people and the prominence of shame (and anger) in his makeup. The biographies and psychological studies emphasize Hitler's isolation as a child and adult (Bromberg and Small, 1983; Bullock, 1964; Davidson, 1977; Miller, 1983; Stierlin, 1976; Toland, 1976). As an infant and a youth, he was pampered by his mother. But even as a three-year-old, his relationship with his father was charged with violence, ridicule, and contempt. By the age of six, he was apparently walled off from everyone, including his mother (Bromberg and Small, 1983; Miller, 1983; Stierlin, 1976).

The three most likely candidates for a close relationship were Kubizek, Braun, and Speer. Hitler and Kubizek were companions for three years, beginning when they were both sixteen. Kubizek's memoir of Hitler (1955) showed that his relationship to Hitler was not that of friend but of adoring admirer. Kubizek described Hitler as a compulsive talker, brooking no interruptions, let alone any disagreement. Lacking any other listeners at this age, Hitler used Kubizek as an audience.

Speer, an architect-engineer, was closest to Hitler among his officials during the last years of the war. In an interview after the war, Speer revealed that although he spent countless hours with Hitler there was no personal relationship between them (Bromberg and Small, 1983, 112): "If Hitler had friends, I would have been his friend."

Braun's diary (Bromberg and Small, 1983, pp. 107–108) showed that she came no closer than Kubizek or Speer. For most of her fifteen-year relationship as Hitler's mistress, he attempted to keep her hidden, confining her to her rooms during meetings with others. A few entries suggested the tone of the whole diary. In 1935, when she was twenty-three and Hitler forty-six, she complained that she felt imprisoned, that she got nothing from their sexual relationship, and that she felt desperately insecure: "He is only using me for definite purposes" (Bromberg and Small, 1983, p. 108). Most of the women with whom Hitler had sexual relations either attempted or committed suicide (Bromberg and Small counted six such relationships, with three of them attempting and three completing suicide [1983, p. 125]). Braun made two such attempts.

In 1942, Hitler inadvertently suggested his isolation from Eva. Hearing of the death of one of his officials, Todt, chief of armaments, Hitler said that he was now deprived of "the only two human beings among all those around me to whom I have been truly and inwardly attached: Dr. Todt is dead and Hess has flown away from me!" (Toland, 1976, p. 666). As Bromberg and Small (1983, p. 150) noted, this statement left Braun out entirely, mentioning instead "a remote man who could rarely be induced to sit at Hitler's table and a man he could not bear to converse with, denounced as crazy, and wished dead."

Neither as a soldier nor as a politician did Hitler have close attachments. His experience as an enlisted man in the army during World War I is illustrative. Although he was a dedicated soldier who demonstrated courage in battle, he was a "loner"; he had no intimates. This may be one of the reasons that, although he was decorated for bravery, he was little promoted; after four years, he left the army at the rank of lance corporal, the equivalent of a private first class. In his evaluations, he was described as lacking in leadership.

After becoming the leader of the Nazi Party, he moved no closer to human relationships. A description of his campaign the year before gaining power is representative (Bromberg and Small, 1983, p.108):

> Hitler used superhuman energy to storm every German state by train, car, and the still-novel airplane. Yet he had almost no real contact with people, not even with his associates, who felt they were touring with a performer. He did not permit them to be colleagues on a team and kept them away from any important people, storing information only in his memory. He remained a lone wolf, now even harsher, often jealous, more distant from his senior associates, and contemptuous of them.

Although the adored leader of millions of people, Hitler apparently had no secure bond with anyone.

The other characteristic of Hitler's personality noted by most of the studies was the prevalence of shame and anger. Diagnostic studies (Bromberg and Small, 1983; Miller, 1983; Stierlin 1976) pointed to shame and humiliation as a prominent feature in Hitler's makeup, both as a child and as an adult. Hitler's father, Alois, was a brutal and tyrannical ruler of his family, but his most intense wrath was turned on Adolf, whom he repeatedly beat and humiliated. Hitler's mother, Klara, pampered him, but she did nothing to protect him from his father since she, too, was intimidated by Alois. The studies just mentioned interpreted Hitler's early childhood experiences to be the source of his later aberrations, his temper tantrums, his sadomasochism, and his fanatical anti-Semitism.

Although the earlier studies are useful, they do not solve the puzzle. The discussions of the first issue, Hitler's psychopathology, are compelling enough. The argument about the needs of the German masses is merely plausible, however, since it is generally quite abstract and is supported only in part by actual evidence.

With respect to the third question, the basis of the overwhelming response to Hitler, the arguments are thin; they might be described as being barely plausible.

The existing literature on this question is unconvincing because it lacks not only evidence but also the most rudimentary form of theory and method. The arguments lack a conceptual framework. For this reason, and because they are post hoc, it is unclear how one might choose among the different versions. None of the explanations proposes directions for future research.

My purpose here is to outline a theory linking the charismatic leader's personality and the response of his followers and a method for the analysis of his discourse. In this chapter, I develop a model of the dynamics of emotion within and between leader and followers.

Humiliated Fury as the Key Affect in Hitler's Life

The Swiss psychoanalyst Miller (1983) called attention to what may be the origin of Hitler's psychopathology: the conjunction of the father's physical and emotional violence and the mother's complicity in it. Miller argued that the rage and shame caused by his father's treatment might have been completely repressed because of his mother's complicity. Although she pampered Hitler and professed to love him, she did not protect him from his father's wrath or allow Adolf to express his feelings about it. Klara, as much as Adolf, was tyrannized by her husband but offered only obedience and respect in return. Because of his mother's "love" for him, as a young child Adolf was required not only to suffer humiliation by his father in silence but also to respect him for it, a basic context for repression.

In later years Hitler ([1927] 1943) was to gloss over his treatment by his parents, which is congruent with repression. He described his father as stern but respected, his childhood as that of a "mother's darling living in a soft downy bed" (Bromberg and Small, 1983, p. 40). However, Alois's son, Alois Jr., left home at fourteen because of his father's harshness. His son, William Patrick, reported that Alois, Sr. beat Alois, Jr. with a hippopotamus whip. Alois, Jr.'s first wife, Brigid, reported that Alois, Sr. frequently beat the children and, on occasion, Klara (Bromberg and Small, 1983, pp. 32–33).

It would appear that Hitler's early childhood constituted an external feeling trap from which there was no escape. This external trap is the analogue to the internal trap proposed by Lewis (1971): When shame is evoked but goes unacknowledged, it generates intense symptoms of mental illness and/or violence toward self or others. Under the conditions of complete repression that seem to have obtained, Hitler's personality was grossly distorted. His biographies suggest that he was constantly in a state of anger bounded by shame.

One indication of Hitler's continual shame-rage was his temper tantrums. Although in later life some of them may have been staged, there is no question that in most of his tantrums he was actually out of control. His older stepbrother reported that Hitler "was imperious and quick to anger from childhood onward and would not listen to anyone. My stepmother always took his part. He would get the craziest notions and get away with it. If he didn't have his way he got very angry. ... [H]e had no friends, took to no one and could be very heartless. He could fly into a rage over any triviality" (Gilbert, 1950, p. 18). In his teens, Hitler's rages were frequent and intense, evoking such descriptions as "red with rage," "exceedingly violent and high-strung," and "like a volcano erupting" (Kubizek, 1955, p. 34).

Hitler's early shame-proneness was suggested by the slightness of the provocation that triggered rage. Kubizek's memoir provided two examples: on learning that he had failed to win a lottery and on seeing Stephanie with other men. Stephanie was a girl whom Hitler longed to meet but never did. He was infatuated with her but never introduced himself (Bromberg and Small, 1983, pp. 55–56).

The most obvious manifestations of Hitler's shame-proneness occurred after he became chancellor. Although easily the most powerful and admired man in Germany, he was constantly fearful that he would appear ridiculous:

> Before he ventured on a political appearance in a new suit or headgear, he had himself photographed to study its effect. In addition to asking his valet whether he looked the part of the Fuehrer, he would check with Hess the manner of speech he should use on different occasions. His anxieties lest he appear ridiculous, weak, vulnerable, incompetent, or in any way inferior are indications of this endless battle with shame.(Bromberg and Small, 1983, p. 183)

Further manifestations of chronic shame states occurred in his relationships with women and in his sexual relationships. In attempting to interest a woman in himself, "even the presence of other persons would not prevent him from repulsive groveling. [He would] tell a lady that he was unworthy to sit near her or kiss her hand but hoped she would look on him with favor. ... One woman reported that after all kinds of self-accusations he said that he was unworthy of being in the same room with her"(Bromberg and Small, 1983, p. 183).

Bromberg and Small (1983, pp. 243–247) went to great lengths to establish that Hitler was never able to have a normal sexual relationship with a woman. Instead, he practiced a type of perversion in which both he and his partner were humiliated. Although the humiliation of the partner was not explicitly described, Hitler's part was: He first required that the partner squat over his face. After a lengthy inspection of her genitals, he demanded that she urinate on his face. Apparently this was the only way he could achieve satisfaction.

These latter descriptions of Hitler's shame states suggest overt, undifferentiated shame, emotionally painful states involving feelings of inadequacy and inferiority. How then are we to understand the other side of Hitler's personality: his arrogance, boldness, and extreme self-confidence? How could a man so prone to shame also be so shameless?

Lewis's concept of the bimodal nature of shame states may provide the answer to this puzzle. In addition to overt shame states, Hitler also had a long history of bypassed shame. Many aspects of his behavior suggested bypassed shame, but I review only three: his temper tantrums, his "piercing stare" (Bromberg and Small, 1983, p. 309), and his obsessiveness.

As already indicated, shame theory suggests that protracted and destructive anger is always generated by unacknowledged shame. Normal anger when not intermixed with shame is usually brief, moderate, and constructive, serving to call notice to adjustments needed in a relationship (Retzinger, 1991). Long chains of shame and anger alternating are experienced as blind rage, hatred, or resentment if the shame component is completely repressed. In this case, the expression of anger serves as a disguise for the hidden shame, projecting onto the outside world the feelings that go unacknowledged within. According to Lewis (1971, p. 85), many "would rather turn the world upside down than turn themselves inside out." This idea exactly captures the psychology of Hitler's lifelong history of intense rage states and his projection of his inner conflict onto scapegoats.

The second indicator of bypassed shame was Hitler's demeanor, especially the nature of his gaze. As early as sixteen, it was described as "blank" or "cruel" (Bromberg and Small, 1983, p. 51). Yet later descriptions (p. 21) said he had "an evasive manner," was "shy" and "never look[ed] a person in the eye," except when he was talking politics (p. 70). These descriptions suggest that Hitler may have been in a virtually permanent state of shame, manifested as either bypassed shame (the stare) or overt shame (avoidance of eye contact). As his power increased, the bypassed mode was more and more in evidence in the form of arrogance, extreme self-confidence, isolation, and obsession.

According to Lewis, the rapidity of speech and behavior that is the prime outer indicator of bypassed shame is usually accompanied by a primary inner manifestation, obsessiveness. Persons in a state of chronic shame may avoid and deny emotional pain by obsessive preoccupation. Hitler's principal obsession, "the Jewish problem," was particularly indicative of unacknowledged shame. At the center of Hitler's belief system was the concept of racial superiority, i.e., that the Aryan race was the superior race; the Jewish "race," the inferior one. His many obsessions with superiority-inferiority, racial purity, pollution, and contamination can be interpreted as operations for bypassing shame. My discussion now shifts from biographical to textual evidence supporting the conjecture that Hitler was motivated by unconscious shame.

Shame-Anger Sequences in *Mein Kampf*

Hitler's book, *Mein Kampf*, was written during his imprisonment after a failed attempt to overthrow the government of Bavaria in 1923. The first half of the book is part autobiography, part history of the Nazi Party. The second half describes the program of the party. Although indications of shame and anger occur throughout, they are the most prevalent in the latter half. The most frequent sequence is the progression from shame to pride. Here is one example, in his discussion of "scientific education" (p. 427):

> There is ground for pride in our people only if we no longer need be ashamed of any class. But a people, half of which is wretched and careworn, or even depraved, offers so sorry a picture that no one should feel any pride in it. Only when a nation is healthy in all its members, in body and soul, can every man's joy in belonging to it rightfully be magnified to that high sentiment which we designate as national pride. And this highest pride will only be felt by the man who knows the greatness of his nation.

There is a reference to pride in each of the four sentences is this passage but only one to shame (the word *ashamed* in the first sentence). This pattern is characteristic: an initial reference to shame followed by repetitive references to pride. One intimation seems to be that, although now ashamed, in the future we will be proud, but only if the Nazi program is carried out. This pattern also suggests the denial of shame, which is mentioned only once, compared to the repeated references to pride, a more "respectable," i.e., less shameful, emotion.

The meaning of the passage is also of interest because it may imply proneness to shame. The phrase "any pride" at the end of the second sentence suggests that if a group has *any* reason for shame, then *all* pride is lost. A more normal response would be that we always have reason for both pride and shame; that is the human condition.

In the passage just quoted the references to pride and shame are explicit. In the following passage, which has the same structure, the references are indirect (p. 411):

> Particularly our German people which today lies broken and defenseless, exposed to the kicks of all the world, needs that suggestive force that lies in self-confidence. This self-confidence must be inculcated in the young national comrade from childhood on. His whole education and training must be so ordered as to give him the conviction that he is absolutely superior to others. Through his physical strength and dexterity, he must recover his faith in invincibility of his whole people. For what formerly led the German army to victory was the sum of the confidence which each individual had in himself and all together in their leadership. What will raise the German people up again is confidence.

Again there is a progression from shame to pride, with a single reference to shame followed by repeated references to pride, but this time both feelings are evoked obliquely. In the first sentence, there is an image of the German people "exposed to the kicks of all the world." Although the word *shame* is not used, the image is clearly one of gross humiliation, of being subject to a humiliating assault by anyone and everyone.

As in the first example, the statement moves very quickly from shame to many references to pride. This time, however, like the reference to shame, those to pride are indirect, using the cognates "self-confidence" and "confidence" rather than "pride" itself. This passage, in addition to containing three more references to confidence, also contains two additional pride cognates, a conviction of "superiority to others" and "faith in invincibility." This pattern, like that in the first passage, is suggestive of the denial of shame since reference to it is quickly negated by many references to pride. The entire passage, and many others, is suggestive of the denial of emotions since shame and pride are referred to only indirectly.

Although there are direct references to pride throughout the book, there are many more indirect references. In addition to those already mentioned, self-confidence, honor, superiority, and faith in one's invincibility, Hitler also frequently invokes "dignity" (and being "worthy") as valued characteristics: "[The task of the 'folk-state'] is not to preserve the decisive influence of an existing social class, but to pick the most capable kinds from the sum of all the national comrades and bring them to office and *dignity*"(p. 431). This passage contains both of the key elements in Hitler's appeal, community and pride; it negates social class in the interest of community and promises prideful office to the most capable, regardless of background.

Most of the manifestations of pride and shame are disguised, requiring reading between the lines. The emotional content of the following passage (p. 390) would be invisible unless one realized that the basic shame context is seeing one's self negatively in the eyes of the other (Sartre, 1956; Lewis, 1971): "How terrible is the damage indirectly done to our Germanism today by the fact that, due to the ignorance of many Americans, the German-jabbering Jews, when they set foot on American soil, are booked to our German account. Surely no one will call the purely external fact that most of this lice-ridden migration from the East speaks German a proof of their German origin and nationality." In this passage, Hitler seems to be seeing himself (and the German people) negatively in the eyes of the other, the American people. Because the shameful (lice-ridden) Jewish immigrants speak German, Americans denigrate Germans and Germany. In the second sentence, he goes on to protest the injustice of the situation produced by his imagination. There is a gratuitous element to this passage that is difficult to define, but it captures the kind of emotional aura that is characteristic of Hitler's prose; it is shame-haunted.

In *Mein Kampf* there are many manifestations of shame, but they are virtually always hidden in encoded terms. Hitler repeatedly refers to disgrace, lack of self-confidence, inferiority, and phrases such as "bowing and scraping" (p. 625) in describing the German people or their representatives. Frequently, shame manifestations are even more indirect, as in the passage just quoted about the "German-jabbering Jews." One of Hitler's frequent themes is the lack of respect for Germany by other nations: "Will any [nation ally itself with] a state ... whose characteristic way of life consists only in *cringing* submissiveness without and *disgraceful* oppression of national virtues within; ... with governments which can boast of *no respect* whatsoever on the part of their citizens, so that foreign countries cannot possibly harbor any greater admiration for them? No, a power which itself wants to be *respected* ... will not ally itself to present-day Germany" (p. 621).

Not only Hitler's statement but also his actions were haunted by the specter of shame. Bromberg and Small (1983, p. 119) noted in passing Hitler's obsession with giantism, with building bigger than anyone. He explained to the workers on one of his building projects, "Why always the biggest? I do this to restore to each individual German his *self-respect*. ... I want to say to the individual: We are not *inferior*; on the contrary, we are the complete equals of every other nation" (Speer, 1970, pp. 69, 107). Because the references to pride and shame were in code language, Bromberg and Small missed their significance. A huge part of Germany's resources, even during wartime, were devoted to the attempt to make Hitler and his followers feel large (proud) rather than small (ashamed).

The primary manifestation of shame in Hitler's behavior was not in construction, however, but in destruction. As Lewis's theory predicts, an individual in a state of chronic shame is very likely to perceive the source of this feeling as an attack by another, generating rage toward that other. Lewis's theory suggests that protracted rage always has its source in unacknowledged shame. In her theory, unacknowledged shame is the cause of destructive aggression because it generates blind rage.

The sequence (unacknowledged shame—rage—aggression) can be traced in particular passages in *Mein Kampf* as well as in the thrust of the book as a whole. The following passage is representative. In one of many attacks on the Treaty of Versailles, after describing it as an instrument of "abject humiliation," he stated, "How could every single one of these points have been burned into the brain and emotion of this people, until finally in sixty million heads, in men and women, a common sense of shame and a common hatred would have become a single fiery sea of flame, from whose heat a will as hard as steel would have risen and a cry burst forth: *Give us arms again!*" (p. 632). In this excerpt, the text moves from humiliation to fury to aggression, the latter step in the form of rearmament for the battle that Hitler prescribed as the destiny of Germany.

What was the battle for which Hitler wanted Germany to prepare? It was a battle against the external and the internal enemy. At first sight it appears that France was the external enemy since he referred many times to the "eternal conflict" between the two countries (e.g., p. 674). He also repeatedly referred to the French motive for destroying Germany, the "thirst for vengeance" (e.g., p. 624), with great indignation, quite oblivious of his own vengefulness. Hitler did not aver revenge as his own motive but is quick to detect it in others; for example, he ascribed to another "hereditary enemy," Negroes, "the perverted sadistic thirst for vengeance" (p. 624).

As becomes apparent quite quickly, however, the ultimate enemy that Hitler saw everywhere was the Jewish people, or, as he put it, the "International Jew." Hitler had a classical ideé fix, a fanatical and unswerving belief. Behind every enemy nation, race, occupation, class, behind every disaster, was the Jewish conspiracy, whose aim was world conquest. Hitler's rage was directed against Jews, whom he confabulated with all other enemies. In Hitler's discourse, capitalists, traitors, revolutionaries, and Marxists were either Jews themselves or in the pay of Jews.

In *Mein Kampf* Hitler's solution to what he called the "Jewish problem" was only slightly disguised. Hitler repeatedly alluded to "the settling of accounts" and a "day of reckoning." In the middle of the last chapter, which has the ominous title "The Right of Emergency Defense," Hitler (p. 679) gave a foretaste of what he had in mind:

> If at the beginning of the War and during the War twelve or fifteen thousand of these Hebrew corrupters of the people had been held under poison gas, as happened to hundred of thousands of our very best German workers in the field, the sacrifice of millions at the front would not have been in vain. On the contrary: twelve thousand scoundrels eliminated in time might have saved the lives of a million real Germans, valuable for the future.

The cycle of shame and rage was focused on a mythical enemy, the Jewish conspiracy and those Hitler believed in its pay, but his destructive aggression killed millions of real people.

The Triple Spiral

I have reviewed evidence suggesting that from very early in childhood, Hitler's actions were determined by unacknowledged shame, alternating between overt and bypassed states. This conjecture is congruent both with his lack of personal relationships and his most frequent emotional states: abject humiliation, arrogant dominance (the "drive for power"), and protracted rage. This combination of insecure social bonds and humiliated fury was endemic among the German masses. Although the family system in which Hitler's personality was formed was extreme, many Germans, perhaps a majority, were probably raised in a similar system dominated by a harsh, tyrannical father and a "loving" mother who yielded completely to the father. This system, as Miller (1983) argued, set the stage for extreme repression. In the societywide crisis that began with Germany's defeat in World War I and culminated in the Great Depression, both outer and inner conditions were ripe for an explosion of humiliated fury. Repressed shame and rage were the link between Hitler and the masses. Hitler's statement and manner sanctioned the intense emotional states that were going unexpressed in his public. Although lacking a theoretical framework, Bromberg and Small's (1983, p. 313) analysis came near to this formulation: "The abundant, almost unheard-of expression of hate and rageful anger ... fired [Hitler's] successful orations. ... [He spoke] the unspeakable for them. His practice of touching off hostile emotions rather than conveying mere critical ideas was wildly successful."

Although this summary formulation ignored what I consider to be the causal emotion—unacknowledged shame—an earlier statement (p. 184; emphasis added) concerning the basic source of Hitler's motives included it:

> Hitler's efforts to *deny his shame* and to avoid situations that would make him feel ashamed pervade much of what he said, wrote, and did. ...
>
> He inveighed against anything he considered indicative of weakness, inferiority, or defeat. Himself far from his tall, blonde, trim, lithe, tough, ideal German male, he allied himself with the tough image. He who feared to swim or sit in a boat or on a horse boasted of racial, political, and military superiority, superlative courage, and physical excellence. In writing and speeches he denied his awareness of humiliating weakness with boasts of his "granite hardness," brutality, mercilessness, and unchangeability, all of which he equated with masculinity. Hardness, brutality, mercilessness, and stubborn perseveration also marked his acts.

All that is missing from this statement in order to explain Hitler's appeal is that his public was in a state of chronic shame. Lewis's theory of the shame-rage feeling trap provides a conceptual model for explaining Hitler's behavior, that of the German masses, and the connection between the two. The model is not an abstract one that leaves out the causal chain, the moment-to-moment links between leader and followers, as in psychoanalytic formulations.

The theory proposed here suggests that Hitler and his public were united by their individual and joint states of emotion, a triple spiral of shame-rage (Scheff, 1990; Scheff and Retzinger, 1991; Retzinger, 1991). They were ashamed, angry that they were ashamed, ashamed that they were angry, and so on without limit. Hitler's hold on the masses was that, instead of ignoring or condemning their humiliated fury (the mistake that Carter made in the Iran hostage crisis), he displayed it himself. In this way, as Bromberg and Small suggested, he sanctioned their fury.

My explanation of Hitler's appeal goes further than that of psychoanalytic formulations, however; it explains how Hitler, in justifying the fury of the Germans, would have seemed to them also to mitigate it. His rage and his projection of German shame onto the Jews would have temporarily lessened the level of pain of the average German by interrupting the chain reaction of overt shame and rage. His own behavior and beliefs implied, "You needn't be ashamed of being humiliated and enraged; it's not your fault." The secret of charisma may be exactly this: the emotional, not the cognitive, content of the message. The leader who is able to decrease the shame level of a group, interrupting the contagion of overt shame, no matter how briefly or at what cost, will be perceived as charismatic.

For comparative purposes, this conjecture can be used to explain Reagan's charisma in dealing with the Iran hostage crisis and Carter's lack of it. Reagan's response to the crisis was to get angry: He expressed insult and outrage, much like the average voter. Carter, however, refrained from expressing emotion, counseling patience and rationality. To persons in the grip of humiliated fury, counsels of this type fail to mitigate their pain or may even increase it; they may feel more ashamed of their shame and anger in the face of advice that seems to deny or condemn them.

In public statements, Carter seemed not only to lack emotion himself but also to deny it in others. Early in the hostage crisis (November 28, 1979) a reporter asked, "How can you satisfy the public demand to end such embarrassment?"(The citations from Carter's and Reagan's press conferences are from Wallace, 1993.) In the main, Carter did not respond at all to the implication that the nation had been embarrassed. Instead he discussed legal and ethical issues in a detached manner. However, at the very end of his statement, he responded to the emotional content of the question in an oblique way, saying that "acts of terrorism may cause *discomfiture* of a people or a government" (p. 34). This response, since it was so distanced, virtually denied all emotion. Discomfiture was a gentilism for shame, but the hypothetical and abstract nature of the phrasing disguised it out of existence.

The most striking aspect of Carter's stance during the crisis was the absence of anger directed at Iran. At no point did he express anger; at most, disappointment and frustration. Like "discomfiture," these words concerned feeling but also disguised and diminish it. Carter seldom expressed emotion, and when he did, it was almost entirely disguised.

Not so his successor. Reagan treated hostile acts by foreign powers as insults, not only to the national honor but to his own. He often responded with anger. The tone was set early in his first term. At the press conference of January 29, 1981, he was asked, "Will your policy toward Iran be one of revenge or reconciliation?" (p. 41.) Reagan's response to this initial question was not emotional: Sounding somewhat like his predecessor, he discussed only legal considerations. By doing so, he first established his moderation and rationality in the face of the temptation toward an emotional response.

His answer to the next question, however, concerning the possibility of U.S. retribution to future terrorism, struck a new note. After first saying that he would not give a specific answer, he went on, "People have gone to bed in some of these countries that have done these things to us in the past confident that they can go to sleep, wake up in the morning, and the United States wouldn't take any action. What I mean by that phrase is that anyone who does these things, violates our rights in the future, is not going to go to bed with that confidence" (p. 40). The emotional style in this passage was quite different from Carter's. Although there was no direct threat, there was an intimation that Reagan might use fire to fight fire. The references to sleeping and waking seemed to threaten night fears to potential terrorists. This passage also suggested self-righteous anger directed at enemies, an emotion that Carter always avoided.

Reagan referred explicitly to this emotion, and also expressed it, in his statement (September 5, 1983) concerning the downing of a Korean jetliner by a Russian fighter: "With our horror and our sorrow, there is a righteous and terrible anger. It would be easy to think in terms of vengeance, but that is not a proper answer" (p. 44). This statement showed a pattern similar to those about the hostage crisis; it expressed righteous anger but denied the propriety of acting on the basis of that emotion. By this maneuver, Reagan managed to suggest both that he was forceful (angry) and that he also was moral since he at least gave the appearance of ruling out vengefulness. He did not, however, give the impression of ignoring or condemning the temptation toward revenge.

Carter's response to insult was to express only the second component, moral righteousness. When asked late in his term (November 2, 1980) about the hostages, he spoke of honor: "Our policy is based on two fundamental objectives, protecting the honor and the vital interests of the United States, and working to insure the earliest possible release of the hostages" (p. 42).

Carter's idea of honor was quite different from Reagan's. Carter indicated later in the same statement that he would use only those means that would uphold the "national honor ... and integrity." Honor for Reagan meant removing dishonor by meeting force with force, but for Carter it meant prudence and moral virtue.

In this instance, Carter urged restraint rather than yielding to the demands for force and retaliation. His counsel of restraint gave him anticharisma and alienated the majority of the voters. Even though his tactics ultimately proved successful, he got little credit. His management of the crisis left an image of weakness and a residue of angry feeling directed toward him. By contrast, when faced with public outcry against Libyan terrorism several years later, Reagan bombed Tripoli. Carter ignored and by implication condemned the emotion trap of the majority of voters (humiliation-rage-aggression); Reagan capitulated to it.

In modern alienated societies, leaders face the dilemma illustrated by Carter's and Reagan's management of emotions. If they resist the shame-anger spiral of the public, they run the danger of losing power, as Carter did. But if they give in to it, they endanger world peace and further the process of self- and social alienation, as Reagan did in regard to Libya and Iran and as Hitler did throughout his career. Perhaps the wiser course would be to acknowledge public emotion, as Reagan did, but avoid acting on it, as Carter did.

Conclusion

This chapter has outlined a way of connecting Hitler to the mass of Germans. I propose that both Hitler and his public were in a state of chronic emotional arousal, a chain reaction of shame and anger, giving rise to humiliated fury. The shame component took the bypassed form, which resulted in a cycle generating rage and destructive aggression since the shame component was not adequately acknowledged.

Because I have sought to solve the problem of Hitler's appeal to the German masses, I have focused considerable attention on Hitler's personality. I want to emphasize, however, that my analysis does not imply that destructive conflict is solely the product of a unique individual like Hitler, a reduction of historical causation to psychological individualism. On the contrary, as has already been suggested in my analysis, Hitler was only a part of a larger system of causation, one that transcended particular individuals, no matter how gifted or depraved. To underscore this point, I want to review the larger historical setting in which Hitler rose to power.

As already indicated, the foundation for Hitler's rise to power was laid by the treatment Germany received at the end of World War I at the hands of the victors. The terms that the Treaty of Versailles imposed on Germany were not conciliatory; they were punitive. The punishment was not only material but also symbolic. The blame placed on Germany as the sole originator of the war was a case in point. The exclusion of Germany from the League of Nations as unworthy was another. These two actions served to formally label and stigmatize Germany, isolating it from the world community. Simmel suggested that conflict may have its roots in separation; material and symbolic exclusion may generate violence.

I can now further link the argument in Chapter 4 with the one in this chapter. The two world wars were interrelated stages of a developing chain of shame and anger. The loss of Alsace-Lorraine represented to most of the French a stain on the national honor, that is to say, it was felt to be shaming. Goodspeed's assessment (1977, p. 6) is now held among a substantial minority of historians: "The French, humiliated and vengeful, could not reconcile themselves to the loss of past glories and were continually reminded of their shame by the 'living wound' of the two lost provinces."

This judgment brings us back to the core of my argument. For much of the period from 1871 to 1914, revanche was a watchword in French politics, helping to bring about World War I. French aggression and vindictiveness toward Germany, which prevailed over Wilson's advocacy of a conciliatory peace, were an emotional response to feelings of humiliation at France's earlier defeat by Germany. World War II was a result of the Treaty of Versailles, just as World War I was a result of the Treaty of Frankfort in 1871. France and Germany were entangled in an interminable conflict driven by unacknowledged shame on both sides.

The aggression by Germany that led to the World War II was not only a product of Hitler's unique personality; it also derived from the unacknowledged alienation in the civilization of that time and the chain reactions of unacknowledged shame and rage that alienation produced and reflected. This lack of attunement between nations was exemplified by the gross miscalculations of all the contenders concerning the cost and duration of World War I. Both sides were convinced that they would win quickly and easily in less than five months and with little loss of life. The Allies thought they would win because they had more armaments and many more troops; the Central powers, because they had better armaments and vastly better planning and organization. Each side demonstrated utter lack of understanding and misunderstanding of the other.

The lack of attunement both between and within nations can be exemplified by the role that England played in the maneuvering that led to World War I. The leaders of England were apparently uncertain as to whether they would fight in a war between France and Germany until the very moment that mobilization began on the Continent. Although the English and French General Staffs had been cooperating in planning a war against Germany, this cooperation was kept secret not only from Germany and the world at large but also from the English themselves; not even the English cabinet was informed. Uncertainty as to whether England would fight seems to have been one of the factors in the German willingness to fight. Had English determination been clear, the German government might have been less aggressive following Sarajevo.

The European nations in the period 1870–1945 bore a strong resemblance to the dysfunctional families described by theorists of family systems (e.g., Bowen, 1978). Conflicts in these families are interminable because of alienation between and within family members. Each is deceptive toward the other not only out of malice, but also, perhaps more significantly, out of self-deception; each family member has disguised or denied his or her own core feelings and needs. The family of nations in our civilization was, and apparently still is, dysfunctional; lack of attunement between and within nations sets the stage for the humiliation-rage-aggression cycle.

This chapter points to the need for further studies of charisma within a micro-macro, part/whole framework. Many studies of World War I are still focused on the single issue of war guilt; a continuing debate on this issue is being waged, particularly in Germany, the United States, and France. Although understanding the role of the various powers in the instigation of the war is a legitimate problem, it is also a very narrow one that ignores many important issues. A viewpoint that relates parts to wholes in the national-international *system* suggests two large and crucial issues:

1. To what extent are studies of war guilt a part of the problem rather than a part of the solution? The blaming that goes on in dysfunctional families is virtually always one of the causes of interminable conflict: each side blames the other, often in a way that insults (humiliates and angers), which continues the cycle of unconscious vengeance. To what extent are studies of war guilt a continuation, by scholarly means, of the war itself?

2. To what extent do studies that focus on only one party to a conflict (either an individual like Hitler or Poincaré or a nation like Germany or France) divert attention from the whole system of which the individual or nation is only a part? It is possible that the narrow focus on individuals or single nations is an unconscious means of protecting the reigning status quo, the overall relationships within and between nations, little changed in basic ways in the last hundred years.

The present world system is based on carefully regulated relationships within nations and virtual anarchy between them. The framework developed in this book suggests that both sets of bonds may be inadequate. The relationships within nations involve too much mutual dependence (engulfment), and those between nations involve too little (isolation). If Simmel and the other theorists quoted here were right, this system will inevitably lead to perpetual conflict. Until we see the system clearly and as a whole, we may continue to repeat the mistakes of the past. The next chapter will focus on directions that might lead us out of this trap.

References

Bowen, M. 1978. *Family Therapy in Clinical Practice.* New York: Jason Aronson.

Bowlby, J. 1969. *Attachment.* New York: Basic Books.

_____. 1973. *Separation.* New York: Basic Books.

_____. 1980. *Loss.* New York: Basic Books.

Braithwaite, J. 1989. *Crime, Shame, and Reintegration.* Cambridge: Cambridge Univ. Press.

Bromberg, N., and V. Small. 1983. *Hitler's Psychopathology.* New York: International Universities Press.

Bullock, A. 1964. *Hitler: A Study in Tyranny.* New York: Harper and Row.

Burlingham, D., and A. Freud. 1942. *Young Children in Wartime London.* London: Allen and Unwin.

Cooley, C. 1922. *Human Nature and the Social Order.* New York: Scribner's.

Dahrendorf, R. 1967. *Society and Democracy in Germany.* Garden City, NY: Doubleday.

Davidson, E. 1977. *The Making of Adolf Hitler.* New York: Macmillan.

Ekman, P., W. Friesen, and P. Ellsworth. 1972. *Emotion in the Human Face.* New York: Pergamon Press.

Gilbert, G. 1950. *The Psychology of Dictatorship.* New York: Ronald Press.

Goffman, E. 1967. *Interaction Ritual.* Garden City, NY: Anchor Books.

Goodspeed, D. J. 1977. *The German Wars: 1914–1945.* Boston: Houghton Mifflin.

Gottschalk, L., C. Wingert, and C. Gleser. 1969. *Manual of Instruction for Using the Gottschalk-Gleser Content Analysis Scales.* Berkeley and Los Angeles: Univ. of California Press.

Hitler, A. [1927] 1943. *Mein Kampf.* Boston: Houghton Mifflin.

Kohut, H. 1971. "Thoughts on Narcissism and Narcissistic Rage." In *The Search for the Self.* New York: International Universities Press.

Kubizek, A. 1955. *The Young Hitler I Knew.* Boston: Houghton Mifflin.

Labov, W., and D. Fanshel. 1977. *Therapeutic Discourse.* New York: Academic Press.

Lasswell, H. 1960. *Psychopathology and Politics.* New York: Viking Press.

Lewis, H. B. 1971. *Shame and Guilt in Neurosis.* New York: International Universities Press.

_____. 1976. *Psychic War in Men and Women.* New York: New York University Press.

_____. 1981. *Freud and Modern Psychology. Vol. 1. The Emotional Basis of Mental Illness.* New York: Plenum Press.

_____. 1983. *Freud and Modern Psychology. Vol. 2: The Emotional Basis of Human Behavior.* New York: Plenum Press.

Marx, Karl. 1975. *Early Writings*. New York: Vintage Books.

Miller, A. 1983. *For Your Own Good*. New York: Farrar, Straus, and Giroux.

Mitchell, O. 1983. *Hitler over Germany*. Philadelphia: Institute for the Study of Human Issues.

Retzinger, S. M. 1991. *Violent Emotions: Shame and Rage in Marital Quarrels*. Newbury Park, CA: Sage.

Sartre, J. 1956. *Being and Nothingness*. New York: Philosophical Library.

Scheff, T. J. 1987. "Interminable Quarrels: Shame-Rage as a Social and a Psychological Spiral." In H. B. Lewis (ed.), *The Role of Shame in Symptom Formation*. Hillsdale, NJ: Erlbaum.

———. 1988. "Shame and Conformity: The Deference-Emotion System." *American Sociological Review* 53: 395–406.

———. 1989. "Cognitive and Emotional Conflict in Anorexia: Re-analysis of a Classic Case." *Psychiatry* 52: 148–163..

———. 1990. *Microsociology: Discourse, Emotion, and Social Structure*. Chicago: Univ. of Chicago Press.

Scheff, T., S. Retzinger, and M. Ryan. 1989. "Crime, Violence and Self-Esteem: Review and Proposals." In A. Mecca, N. Smelser, and J. Vasconcellos (eds.), *The Social Importance of Self-Esteem*. Berkeley and Los Angeles: Univ. of California Press.

Speer, A. 1970. *Inside the Third Reich*. New York: Macmillan.

Stierlin, H. 1976. *Adolf Hitler: A Family Perspective*. New York: Psychohistory Press.

Toland, J. 1976. *Adolf Hitler*. Garden City, NY: Doubleday.

Waite, R. 1977. *The Psychopathic God: Adolf Hitler*. New York: Basic Books.

Wallace, G. M. 1993. "Competition and Rules of Discourse in Presidential News Conferences." Ph.D. diss., University of California, Santa Barbara.

Watzlawick, P., J. H. Beavin, and D. Jackson. 1967. *The Pragmatics of Human Communication*. New York: Norton.

PART THREE

Conclusion

6

Acknowledgment
and Reconciliation

Though with their high wrongs I am struck to the quick,
Yet with my nobler reason against my fury
Do I take part. The rarer action is
In virtue than in vengeance. They being penitent,
The sole drift of my purpose doth extend
Not a frown further.

—Shakespeare, *The Tempest*, Act 5, Scene 1, lines 24–30

The preceding chapters proposed that unacknowledged alienation and shame cause interminable conflict. This final chapter deals with two limitations of this approach. The first is that in focusing on shame, it excludes consideration of other emotions, such as grief, fear, and anxiety, which may also play a role in conflict. The second limitation concerns the concept of acknowledgment. This idea plays a crucial role in my theory, but it has not yet been clearly explained. The main emphasis in this chapter is on unpacking the concept of acknowledgment and suggesting how it might help with the vast problem of reconciliation between nations.

I first review the work of Goffman and Tavuchis on remedial actions, with special emphasis on the sociology and psychology of apologies. I propose that successful apologies require acknowledgment of feelings. To show that even a slight difference in the degree of acknowledgment of shame might make a substantial difference in social actions, I compare two incidents of the management of shame, one in French, the other in German history (1871–1945).

The next step is to apply the idea of acknowledgment to the problem of reconciliation between nations. I first discuss some long-range directions toward peace. The last section of this chapter concerns two more immediate issues: the kind of mediation that might decrease the risk of war and forms of "lustration" (a collective ritual of purification) that may be needed in the aftermath of war and other social upheavals. These two issues correspond to the two poles of bimodal alienation. I hypothesize that interminable conflict is caused by alienation between and within disputing groups. Effective mediation to prevent war would attempt to repair damaged bonds between nations before they resort to war; collective rituals of purification (lustration) would help repair divisions within nations in the aftermath of war.

To give a current example of the need for lustration: The division among the Serbs, Croats, and Muslims in the nation that was formerly Yugoslavia was not healed after World War I, or after World War II. This division continues to be the main cause of interminable conflict in this region. But first I provide a discussion of the problem of including other emotions in the analysis of conflict.

Grief, Anger, Fear, and Anxiety

As already indicated, I believe that emotions additional to shame and anger play a role in causing wars. Grief, anger, fear, and anxiety are frequently mentioned as causes of aggression and conflict. Freud, in his comments on aggression, usually pointed to anxiety as a cause. In the case of verbal wit and aggression, he seemed to think of unconscious anger as causal. As already indicated, Gaylin (1984) suggested that fear is as important as shame in causing violence. Mitscherlich and Mitscherlich (1975) and Volkan (1988) proposed that unresolved grief can lead to collective aggression.

The main problem involved in these and similar theories of the role of particular emotions in generating conflict is the absence of explicit theory and method. Each of these earlier conjectures singled out a single causal emotion without specifying the causal chain of which it is a part. How is each of these emotions positioned with the matrix of perception, thought, and behavior of each party to a conflict, and how is it located with respect to the interaction of the parties? In the case of anger, for example, my approach suggests that it causes conflict only in the presence of shame.

Just as these earlier formulations lacked an explicit theoretical framework, they also lacked clearly described methods. No concepts were defined, and few examples were offered. When examples were provided, they were not systematically analyzed. For this reason, these earlier discussions of emotion and aggression lacked a sense of being grounded in data or even oriented to the possibility of how one would obtain data that would lead to support and modification. Lacking theory and method, these formulations were so primitive as to be of little help in systematic research on conflict.

I have attemped to detect grief, anger, fear, and anxiety in verbal and nonverbal cues, but without much success. Both Ekman and Friesen (1978) and Izard (1979) provided very detailed procedures for detecting grief, anger, and fear in facial expression. In the eleven videotapes and audiotapes of interpersonal conflict Retzinger and I studied, we noticed moments of sadness or grief. But these moments were infrequent, brief, and located in such a way that little relationship to conflict was suggested. We found no indications of fear whatsoever. However, the absence of fear was probably due to the nature of our sample since there was no physical violence in any of our cases.

Finding emotions in verbal texts is still more difficult. The Gottschalk-Gleser (1969) procedure for coding anxiety, hostility, and alienation provides an example of the problem. This system offers no scale for grief or fear. But for anxiety there are six different subscales: death, mutilation, separation, guilt, shame, and nonspecific anxiety. Both Lewis (1971) and Retzinger (1991) used the Gottschalk-Gleser shame-anxiety scale in their own studies of shame without making reference to the anxiety component. Their reticence was understandable: For systematic research, anxiety is a will-of-the-wisp.

The Gottschalk-Gleser procedure confounds subjects that may provoke emotion, death, and mutilation, and various basic emotions with one another. A review of the items in these scales shows first that fear items are scattered among the death, mutilation, and nonspecific scales. The items in the separation scale suggest serveral emotions but with grief predominant. Similarly, in the guilt and shame anxiety scales, guilt and shame items predominate. The Gottschalk-Gleser anxiety scale is conceptually chaotic.

One obvious difficulty with the concept of anxiety is its vagueness. In usual usage, it has come to mean any kind of ambiguous emotion. Although originally linked only to fear, anxiety has become a miscellaneous category both in popular and professional parlance. For example, the phrase *social anxiety* is a disguised reference to embarrassment or shame.

Miscellaneous categories are abstractions that preclude the necessity of saying actual names. Anxiety fills such a function in modern discourse. Until recently in psychoanalyisis, there had been little discussion of shame; shame and other emotions were included in the grab bag of anxiety. The concept of emotional arousal fills a similar role in behaviorist approaches, which also usually exclude considerations of shame. In modern societies, emotions are treated as residual categories, even by most psychoanalysts and social scientists. The idea that anxiety leads to conflict is equivalent to saying that it is caused by tension, a formulation leading nowhere.

Gottschalk et al. did not include a fear or grief subscale, and their cues for anxiety were so diverse and far-ranging that they seemed to apply to all emotions. Falling back on my own devices, I saw no evidence of grief, fear, or anxiety in any of the texts on the world wars that I examined. Perhaps some usable method for detecting these emotions will be devised, but at this time I have found no way to show that they play a role in destructive conflict.

Nevertheless, I believe that unresolved fear and grief are probably causal emotions in conflict, along with shame. In my approach, however, these emotions are located within the causal chain in such a way as to be secondary to shame, just as anger is secondary. My theory proposes that unacknowledged shame is the agent of repression: It is shame that leads to forgetting of thoughts and feelings. This formulation is suggested in Freud's earliest work ([1896] 1961, p. 268; emphasis added): "[The memories, ideas, and feelings that are repressed are] all of a distressing nature calculated to arouse the affect of *shame*, of self-reproach, psychical pain, and the feeling of being harmed." As in Freud's comment, which in his later work he seemed to forget, in my approach shame is the master emotion in that it determines whether other emotions will be felt and discharged or repressed.

Given this view, I agree that unresolved grief and fear may cause conflict. But in the theory proposed here, shame is the cause of the lack of resolution of these emotions. When there is no unacknowledged shame, we feel and discharge grief through weeping and fear through shaking and sweating and other cathartic processes, such as discussing our emotions. Perhaps the function of fundamental collective rituals, such as those of mourning, is to remove the shame of discharging these emotions (Scheff, 1979).

The Concept of Acknowledgment

One implication of the preceding chapters is that acknowledgment of alienation and shame within and between nations would be a vital step toward a peaceful world. This formulation exposes a large gap in my approach and in that of Lewis, whose work I draw on: the absence of adequate conceptualization and exploration of the process of acknowledgment. Lewis's (1971) theory and research were entirely concerned with shame that was denied and disguised. She did not spell out the meaning of acknowledgment or offer any examples of its occurence. As already mentioned in Chapter 3, acknowledgment is an abstraction that is difficult to explicate and apply. The earlier chapters in this book were concerned with instances of the complete denial of alienation-shame. Even to understand these instances, it would be helpful to explicate the concept of acknowledgment and offer examples of what it looks like in discourse.

The part/whole method implies the need for comparisons, especially between extremes. The concept of alienation needs to be understood in comparison with its opposite, solidarity. In a similar way, pride and shame are also such a pair. We understand concepts in the context of other concepts, especially polar opposites. All concepts imply a larger theory, but one that is seldom made explicit.

The use of "limiting conditions" by mathematicians is an example of part/whole comparisons. To move quickly toward understanding the implications of a complex equation, we observe its behavior at its two extremes: zero and infinity. To understand how entrapped nations were in the social system of which they were a part prior to the two world wars, we need to imagine what a social system might be like if the nations were able to escape the trap. Just as instances of denial help us understand the meaning of acknowledgment, instances of acknowledgment help understand the meaning of denial. One issue among many that needs to be explored is the relationship between acknowledgment of alienation-shame and the naming of these states. Does putting feeling states into words help dispel them or at least decrease their destructive consequences? Perhaps, but only under the right conditions.

Hitler's derogatory phrase for the Weimar Republic, mentioned in Chapter 5, provides an instance: "Fourteen years of shame and disgrace!" He named the collective feelings that other leaders ignored but not in a way that would help dispel those feelings. He used the naming of the emotion of shame in an enraged attack on others rather than as an expression of what he himself was feeling in the moment. This instance suggests that for the naming of a feeling to be part of a process of acknowledgment, there needs to be *congruence* between verbal and nonverbal expression.

No such congruence is present in the Hitler example. Although he was naming the emotion of shame, he was expressing anger and contempt with his nonverbal gestures. The idea of congruence between outer and inner expression is widely accepted by psychotherapists as a sign of mental health. It is also implied in Tavuchis's rule for genuine apology.

In terms of the theory proposed here, the most prominent emotion expressed by Hitler in his use of this phrase, his table-pounding rage, was itself a denial of his own shame. Rather than expressing his feelings about Germany's inferiority and rejection by the world community, he disguised them behind an angry and imperious facade.

Apologies

Reconciliation—the repairing of a disruption in a social relationship—can be seen as an acknowledgment of interdependence. Viewed in this way, apologies, the most concentrated path to the repair of social bonds, expose many of the key elements in conflict and reconciliation. Describing the components of the ritual of apology may be a succinct way of beginning to unpack the concept of acknowledgment.

The two leading theorists of apology and reconciliation are Goffman and Tavuchis. Goffman (1971) considered apology in his treatment of remedial and reparative devices. Even though his discussion of apologies was quite brief, it bristled with ideas (p. 113; emphasis added):

> In its fullest form, the apology has several elements: expression of *embarrassment and chagrin*; clarification that one knows what conduct had been expected and sympathizes with the application of negative sanction; verbal rejection, repudiation, and

disavowal of the wrong way of behaving along with vilification of the self that so behaved; espousal of the right way and an avowal henceforth to pursue that course; performance of penance and the volunteering of restitution.

Two aspects of this long sentence catch the eye. First, in a few lines, Goffman loaded in not one or two but *eight* necessary elements for a successful apology, a monument to concision. Second, the first element of an apology that Goffman invoked was "expression of embarrassment and chagrin," which connects his argument to mine concerning pride and shame. Moreover, placing this element at the head of the list suggested not only that it should come first in time but also that it might be the most important condition.

Goffman's discussion has proven fruitful in many directions, but it has also been sharply criticized by Tavuchis (1991), whose discussion of apologies was much more comprehensive and detailed than Goffman's. Although Tavuchis praised Goffman's discussion, he was also critical of Goffman's entire approach to remedial actions. Unlike Goffman, Tavuchis readily extended his analysis beyond interpersonal apology to individual-collective and collective remedial actions. He devoted chapter-length treatments to situations of apology of the one to the many, the many to the one, and the many to the many. In his treatment of interactions between individuals and groups, he covered some of the same ground as Braithwaite (1989), but in much more detail. The ceremonies of punishment and reintegration of offenders that Braithwaite described involve the repair of bonds between the one and the many, which Tavuchis discussed in great detail. Of particular relevance to this chapter is Tavuchis's discussion of apologies of the many to many: the path to reconciliation between groups.

Tavuchis's (1991, p. 138) two central complaints about Goffman's treatment of apologies were that in the main it concerned individuals, rather than relationships, and that to these individuals an apology may be a game in which the actor is not emotionally involved: "apologies [for Goffman] are conceptualized as a 'set of moves' or interpersonal management ploys used by socially disembodied actors trying to maximize their (questionable) moral credibility. ... Goffman argues that an apology entails the 'splitting' of the self, whereas I underscore the necessity of 'attachment' to the offense. ... *There is no mention of what I take to be central to apology: sorrow and regret.* ... An actor could follow all the steps described by Goffman without producing a speech act that is socially recognizable as an apology, or, its moral reciprocal, forgiveness." I believe that both of Tavuchis's criticisms cut close to the bone. Although Goffman used many relational terms, his basic frame of analysis was individualistic rather than relational; it concerned a harried, anxious individual seeking to maintain her or his sense of self and status in a jungle of trying situations. The language of rules and norms, which Tavuchis also used, is itself not quite relational since it also emphasizes the individual as much as the social bond. (Perhaps a new language of relationships is needed. In the physics of light, mathematical language provided the link between particle and wave formulations. We have no such language for linking individuals and relationships.)

Goffman's analysis was also largely behavioral; it concerned the surface of interaction, with very little access to the interior, the meaning of events to the actors. Even Goffman's mention of embarrassment and chagrin as necessary parts of apology involved a fatal ambiguity. He did not say that the actor should *feel* these emotions, only that she or he should express them. In Goffman's world, a gesture indicating embarrassment (covering the face with a hand, for example) might be adequate, even if it was merely enacted in the absence of any feeling (as when addressing an audience, Ulysses would wipe his eyes with the hem of his robe to indicate grief). In Tavuchis's (1991, p. 31) description of the ritual of apology, there are two essential parts: One must *say* one is sorry, and one must also *feel* sorry. Without these two components, the ritual is incomplete.

To test the adequacy of some particular apology, one can invoke what I call "Tavuchis's rule": An apology is genuine to the extent that one both says one is sorry and actually feels sorry. His rule concerns congruence between outer and inner. An actual instance of a defective apology provides an example.

Speer, one of Hitler's chief lieutenants, was tried and convicted of crimes against humanity at Nuremberg. (For earlier commentary on this case, see Scheff and Retzinger, 1991, pp. 180–185.) Unlike any of the other defendants, however, his life was spared. Instead of being executed, he spent twenty-one years in solitary confinement at Spandau prison, outside of Berlin. During this period, he wrote his memoirs. One recurring theme was the regret he expressed about the role he played in Hitler's Germany. In some ways, the book can be read as an apology for his actions.

If the book is an apology, however, it does not seem to be an adequate one; it is frequently off pitch in some essential way. It is true that some of the apologetic statements sound genuine. Tavuchis (1991, p. 21) pointed to an excellent one. But even one false note in a text can call into question the validity of an apology: Perhaps most of the words sound right, but does the person apologizing actually feel sorry? There are many lapses in Speer's memoirs.

In an insightful review, Steiner (1971) described Speer's attempts at apology as "motions, presumably sincere in their own hollow, cerebral way, of retrospective horror." Although Steiner did not provide examples to show how hollow and cerebral Speer's attempts were, they can be easily found in the text. One (Speer, 1970, p. 24) begins with a statment that almost strikes the right note: "By entering Hitler's party I had already, in essence, assumed a responsiblity that led directly to the brutalities of forced labor, to the destruction of war, and to the deaths of those millions of so-called undesireable stock, to the crushing of justice and the elevation of every evil." Even in this passage there is questionable phrasing. But it hints at some feeling of responsibility and remorse. One touch is that Speer heads his list of crimes with "the brutalities of forced labor," a crime in which he was directly implicated as the overseer of the armament industry.

But in the rest of the paragraph, the tone falters: "In 1931 [when he joined the Nazi Party] I had no idea that fourteen years later I would have to answer for a host of crimes to which I subscribed beforehand by entering the party." Although somewhat indirect, this sentence seems to be more of an excuse ("I didn't know") than an apology. It denies his own continuing responsibility for his actions by implying that once he had joined the party, a youthful folly, blind loyalty was inescapable.

The paragraph ends with a whimper: "I did not yet know that I would atone with twenty-one years of my life for frivolity and thoughtlessness and breaking with tradition." There is a thread of self-justification and self-pity running through the entire paragraph, faint at first but dominant in the last sentence. Instead of expressing gratitude that of all the Nuremberg defendants he alone was spared death, he seems to complain about the length of the prison sentence. The most shocking element, however, is the terms used to describe the causes of his adherence to the Nazi Party: "frivolity," "thoughtlessness," and "breaking with tradition." These terms would be appropriate if he had participated in a panty raid, but not in crimes whose scope and vileness beggar the imagination.

Speer's apology fails the second part of the Tavuchis rule. Although Speer said many times that he was sorry, the way he said it suggested that he did not feel sorry. His failure occurred with both cognitive and emotional aspects. In terms of the cognitive content, self-justification is exactly the opposite of what is required in an apology, taking responsibility for one's own actions with no excuses.

Speer's apology also fails to pass at the emotional level. The connotations of many of his words and phrases work against the expression of remorse. One example is the phrase "undesirable stock." Although Speer qualified this phrase with "so-called," it still strikes the wrong note. He was referring to the victims of Nazi atrocities, such as the Jews and Slavs who were murdered or worked to death. To use a term from his Nazi past, rather than from the present day, was an appalling blunder since it suggested that in some ways his point of view, and therefore his feelings, still had not changed. Sustaining the right tone in an apology seems to require actually feeling remorse, the second part of the Tavuchis test.

My discussion of the Speer case suggests that Tavuchis's analysis is helpful in understanding the nature of apology and therefore of acknowledgment of feelings. However, I wish to extend the description of the core ritual of apology further than Tavuchis took it in order to resolve an issue that he left unresolved. In many different passages, Tavuchis puzzled over a mystery: How can mere words resolve conflict? He noted that an apology, however fastidious, does not undo the harmful act. Tavuchis repeatedly indicated that successful apologies are like *magic*. Using only words, one can obtain genuine forgiveness for an injurious act: "Although I have referred frequently to forgiveness as a crucial element in the apologetic equation, this mysterious and unpremeditated faculty has not been adequately addressed or formulated. If, as I have argued, sorrow is the energizing force of apology, then what moves the offended party to forgive? [The] social and psychodynamic *sources* [of forgiveness] have been relatively neglected"(1991, p. 122). The way in which I have treated pride and shame in this book may speak to the issue that Tavuchis raised: What are the social and psychodynamic sources of apology and forgiveness? I deal first with psychodynamic sources, the vicissitudes of emotions and feelings, then with social ones.

Shame and Apology

I agree with the first part of Tavuchis's rule: One must say one is sorry or words to that effect. But to understand the magic of apology and forgiveness, it may be necessary to unpack the second part of the formula, that one must also feel sorry. What are the emotional components of feeling sorry?

In the passage just quoted, Tavuchis stated that *sorrow,* that is, grief, is the energizing force of apology. I disagree. Although feeling and displaying grief may be helpful, it may not be the main emotion required for an apology to accomplish its purpose. I propose that an effective apology requires that the predominant emotion of the party making the apology be one of embarrassment. This is difficult for participants, or even for observers, to see because in our civilization embarrassment and shame are so frequently and deeply disguised and denied as to be rendered almost invisible (Lynd, 1958; Lewis, 1971; Scheff, 1990). Although Tavuchis discussed shame at several points (as in note 4, p. 151), this emotion did not figure prominently in his discussion.

Suppose, for the purpose of argument, after one party has been injured by another, both parties are in a state of embarrassment or shame. Depending on the gravity of the injury, the intensity of shame may range from slight embarrassment to severe and prolonged states of humiliation. The *injured* party may feel helpless, rejected, powerless, or inadequate because of the treatment received; the *injuring* party may feel unworthy because he or she has injured the other. All these terms have been rated as encoded references to shame (Gottschalk and Gleser, 1969; Lewis, 1971). The shared mood of the two parties is bleak; they are in a state of shared embarrassment or shame.

The function of apology under these conditions is to allow both parties to acknowledge and discharge, rather than deny, the burden of shame they are carrying with respect to the injurious act. This function is difficult for the parties to be aware of in Western societies because shame is routinely denied. Perhaps if social psychology brought unacknowledged shame to light, we might be able to understand and increase the magic of apology.

An effective apology is also difficult because it depends on a veritable symphony of verbal and nonverbal activities jointly enacted and felt by both parties. Each must coordinate their words, gestures, thoughts, and feelings with those of the other. It is a dance, a pas de deux, requiring not only the right lyrics but also the right music. That is, the timing (rhythm) of the moves of each party relative to the moves of the other is crucial, as are the emotions displayed (melody) and felt (harmony).

This formulation in terms of emotion dynamics may remove some of the mystery from apology and forgiveness. If the lyrics and the melody of the apologizing party are right, and the attitude of the apologized-to party is accepting, then a dramatic mood change can occur: The parties can go from a state of shared shame to one of shared pride in a matter of minutes, from fluster, awkwardness, and emotional pain to rapport and pleasure.

Social Sources of Apology

Social relationships are difficult to describe in Western societies because human interdependence is routinely denied. Our public discourse is in the language of individuals rather than of relationships. In the earlier chapters I defined a social bond in terms of the mix of solidarity and alienation (see also Scheff, 1990; Retzinger, 1991). A secure bond is a relationship in which solidarity prevails: Accurate understanding by each party of the other's thoughts and feelings, short- and long-term intentions, and character prevails over misunderstanding or lack of understanding. In an insecure or a threatened bond, alienation dominates: Lack of understanding or misunderstanding in these matters occurs on one or both sides. Most social bonds are a mix, but either solidarity or alienation predominates.

As indicated in earlier chapters, alienation occurs in two different formats. A secure bond requires balance between the importance of the individuals and the importance of the relationship (Elias, 1989). Too much emphasis on the individual means isolation; each cannot know the other and reveal the self because both are too distant. Too much emphasis on the relationship means engulfment; each cannot know the other and reveal the self because loyalty and conformity demand that important parts of the self, basic desires, thoughts, and feelings may be hidden, even from the self. Secrecy, deception, and self-deception go hand in hand. Modern societies tend toward individuation and isolation; traditional ones, toward conformity and engulfment. Both formats are equally alienated.

The apology-forgiveness transaction signifies the removal of a threat to the social bond. In relational language, in every moment of every encounter, the bond is either being maintained, strengthened, repaired, or damaged. This is one of Goffman's (1967) central themes: *Every* action (or inaction) by each party has an effect on the relative status and sense of self of the parties.

By verbal and nonverbal means, an effective apology is a masterstroke in this scenario, a repair of a threatened or insecure bond. When one party has injured another, the bond is threatened; the parties are disconnected emotionally and/or cognitively, i.e., they are in a state of shame. A successful apology allows both parties to acknowledge and discharge the shame evoked by the injury. The apology "makes things right" between the parties both emotionally and cognitively; it repairs the breach in the bond. The success of the action of repair is felt and signaled by both parties; they both feel and display the emotion of pride.

Bond language is needed if we are to understand and describe the process of denial and acknowledgment. Acknowledgment of the state of a relationship (the degree of attunement and its accompanying emotions) leads to the building or repair of bonds; denial, to damage to bonds.

Acknowledgment of Shame and Levels of Collective Sanity

Tavuchis's analysis of apology and my commentary on it suggest the complexity of the concept of acknowledgment and of its practice in real life, even at the interpersonal level. At the level of relations between nations, the issues are further complicated by the large number of participants and vastly increased volume of discourse. In the theory proposed here, acknowledgment of interdependence and emotion, the state of the bond, is crucial not only for individuals but also for whole societies. In this section I apply the idea of acknowledgment to two historical instances closely related to the main themes of this book.

The comparison I make is between French nationalism during the Third Republic (1871–1914) and German nationalism during the Weimar-Nazi era (1918–1945). I argue that both nationalisms were shame-driven. Although shame went largely unacknowledged in both cases, it appears there was slightly more acknowledgment in the French case than in the German.

As discussed in Chapter 3, the French public and its leaders experienced their defeat in the Franco-Prussian War (1870–1871), and the Treaty of Frankfurt that ended the war, as humiliating (Kennan, 1984; Sontag, 1933; Weber, 1968). Going against Bismarck's warnings (he feared revenge), the Germans annexed two French provinces (Alsace and Lorraine). Revenge brought about through the return of the two lost provinces, revanchism, although never explicitly acknowledged by the various French governments, became one of the most crucial issues in French politics of the whole era.

The point I want to make about the current of revenge in French politics from 1871 to 1914 is that it was somewhat more overt than its German variant in the period 1918–1945. Leading political figures such as Gambetta and Boulanger talked about revenge openly in their campaigns for public office (Boulanger was known in the popular press as "General Revenge"). Vengeance against Germany was a popular theme in newspapers, magazines, and other political discourse.

The overt use of revenge themes was also reflected in the popular literature of the time. Two examples will suffice. The war poems of Deroulede, who fought in the France-Prussian War, *Chants du soldat* (Songs of a soldier, 1872) were wildly popular. Here is a sample stanza (quoted in Rutkoff, 1981, p. 161):

Revenge will come, perhaps slowly
Perhaps with fragility, yet a strength that is sure
For bitterness is already born and force will follow
And cowards only the battle will ignore.

Note that this poem not only appeals to the French to seek revenge but also contains a coercive element. In the last line, anyone who might disagree with the poet's sentiments is labeled a coward. There are many other instances of appeals to vengeance, honor, and glory in the other poems; these are the main themes. By 1890 this little book had gone through an unprecedented eighty-three editions, which suggests that most everyone in France might have been familiar with it.

The extraordinary acclaim that greeted *Chants du soldat* prompted Deroulede to publish further books of similar thrust, most of them devoted to military glory, triumph, and revenge. For example, in 1896 his *Poesies militaire* (Military poesy) continued in the same vein. The following is a representative stanza (emphasis added):

French blood!—a treasure so august
    And hoarded with such jealous care,
To crush oppression's strength unjust,
With all the force of right robust,
    And *buy us back our honor fair*

Although revenge is not mentioned explicitly, the last line implies what might be called the "honor-insult-revenge cycle" (Scheff and Retzinger, 1991).

Also indicative of open revanchism was the rash of novels about the plight of Alsace and Lorraine under German occupation, which became popular in the fifteen years preceding World War I. The best-known author of this genre, Barres, published two: *Au service de l'Allemagne* (In the service of Germany, 1905) and *Colette Baudoche* (1909). These books, like the many others of their ilk,[1] were not works of art but "works of war," to use the phrase of Barres's biographer, de Boisdeffre (quoted in Doty, 1976, p. 229).

There seemed to have been no comparable explicitness about vengeance in the German nationalism of the Weimar and Nazi eras. Revenge was seldom avowed as a motive of Germany in the popular press or literature. Hitler, the most outspoken of the German nationalists, did not admit to vengeful motives of his own. The word came up often in his speeches and writing, but not as a motive for Germany. Instead he attributed it to the those he proclaimed to be enemies of Germany: the French, Negroes, and Jews.

---

1. Paul Acker's *Les Exiles* (1911), René Bazin's *Oberlé* (1901), L. Dumont-Wilden's *La Victoire des vaincus* (1911), Jeanne Regamy's *Jeune Alsace* (1909), André Lichtenberger's *Juste Lobel alsacien* (1911), Hansi's *Professor Knatsche* (1910) and *Mon village* (1913), Georges Ducrocq's *Les Provinces inébranables* (1913) and *Adrienne* (1914), Etienne Rey's *La Renaissance de l'orgueil française* (1912), and Robert Baldy's *L'Alsace-Lorraine et l'Empire allemand* (1912) (cited in Doty, 1976, p. 229).

As already indicated in Chapter 5, in *Mein Kampf* ([1927] 1943) he frequently referred to the French "thirst for vengeance" (as on p. 624). He also ascribed the same motive to another "hereditary" (i.e., racial) enemy of Germany, the Negroes, attributing to them "the perverted sadistic thirst for vengeance" (p. 624). His speeches and writings also contained similar attributions to Jews.

Although Hitler never explicitly acknowledged his own desire for vengeance, it was often implied in his speeches, writings, and actions. His choice of terminology frequently suggested a hidden revenge motive. For example, in his discussions of the "Jewish problem," he used phrases such as "the day of reckoning" and "the settling of accounts." Such phrases seemed to imply a "balancing of the books" by "paying back," i. e., revenge. His obsession with the humiliation of Versailles also implied revenge. As indicated earlier, he seldom referred to the Weimar government by its actual name. The implication of such discourse was that France and the Allies had insulted and humiliated Germany but that Germany would pay them back in kind.

The motives that Hitler ascribed to himself were either lofty and abstract ("a new world order") or "practical" (*Lebensraum*, "room to live," in explaining his designs on Poland and Russia). His discourse strongly suggested that his actual motives were humiliated fury and the desire for revenge but that he was completely unaware of them, as indicated in Chapter 5. His attribution of the motive of revenge to the French might have been justified, but his view of Negroes and Jews seemed to have been a projection: He denied his own emotions by attributing them to others.

Many currents similar to the German ones can be found in French nationalism and its accompanying anti-Semitism, but at a lower level of delusion and hatred. Even in the writings of the most vitriolic of the French anti-Semites, Edouard Drumont, there was no projection of revenge and no hint of genocide. (Drumont's main work, *La France Juive* [Jewish France, 1886], was very popular, going through forty-three editions by the turn of the century.)

I have proposed that the basic emotional motive for both French and German nationalism was unacknowledged shame and rage but that these emotions were managed somewhat differently in the two groups. Although mostly repressed in French nationalism, these emotions were also partly acknowledged in coded form. Encoded expressions of shame, as indicated in Chapter 2, are not the deepest level of repression. Conceptions of honor, humiliation, and revenge more frequently appeared in French discourse than in German. In my view, this degree of verbal acknowledgment of shame, small that it was, prevented descent into complete madness; merely verbal discourse on revenge would not have been cathartic, but I assume that it was accompanied by nonverbal expression and discharge of shame.

By contrast, in German nationalism shame went virtually unacknowledged. Instead it was denied, rationalized, and projected onto other groups. As suggested in Chapter 2, this is the deepest level of repression; shame is not expressed even in an encoded form. Instead, silence reigns. There is no acknowledgment of one's humiliation at all, not a scintilla. For this reason, I argue, Hitler and the majority of Germans entered into a more or less continuous shame-rage spiral that ended only with the death of Hitler and military defeat. I attribute the fanaticism of Hitler's policies to this cause: A continuing shame-rage spiral means madness, whether for an individual or a group.

Shame and Delusion

French and German legends of the stab in the back during the two periods suggest a French level and a German level of collective delusion. Military defeats often lead to stab-in-the-back legends. One occurred in recent U.S. history when the Chinese Nationalists, a proxy for U.S. military might, were defeated by the Communists. Senator Joseph McCarthy alleged that the United States had "lost China" because of treason by U.S. diplomats, who, he thought, had favored the Communists over the Nationalists. McCarthy's charges had serious repercussions: The Department of State fired two career diplomats because of them. The firings ended the diplomats' careers, but after many years they were exonerated.

A less virulent form of the legend appeared after U.S. defeat in Vietnam. Prominent politicians and high-ranking military officials, including the military leader of the war, General William Westmoreland, did not cry treason, but they did argue that the war was lost because of civilian control over the military effort. After the German defeat in World War I, a similar although much more venomous story, the *Dolchstoss* legend was born.

In its various manifestations, the stab-in-the-back legend is relevant to the argument in this book since it can be taken as a defense against shame. An individual or collective defeat can easily be seen by participants and others as shameful, a dramatic signal of unworthiness or inadequacy. The stab-in-the-back legend is a justification of self or group: It is not our fault, we are worthy, but we were betrayed. When such a falsehood is enshrined as official history, it can be an emblem of complete denial of shame in a society as a whole.

If we return to the period of 1871–1914 in French history, we can compare the Dreyfus case and its outcome to the German *Dolchstoss* legend. Dreyfus was a Jew and a colonel in the French army in the period following the French defeat by the Germans in 1871. He was arrested, tried, and convicted of spying for the Germans. The stab-in-the-back legend was the unstated subtext of the case. The army's fanatical belief in Dreyfus's guilt may have been a defense against the shame of the army's defeat. It was not military weakness and incompetence that lost the war but betrayal.

When crucial evidence was found that another French officer, not a Jew, was the actual spy and that the case against Dreyfus was totally fabricated, the army repeatedly suppressed the new evidence. In contemporary language, there was a massive coverup. The high command seemed to feel that the honor of the army, which it equated with the honor of France, was at stake. After several appeals and further trials, Dreyfus was finally exonerated. But the case precariously divided French society into warring camps of almost equal size and strength.

Although French society was split apart for years over Dreyfus's guilt or innocence, the social fabric held. The public revelation of the army's role in prosecuting Dreyfus on false evidence disgraced several high-ranking officers. In this case, although it was a close call, truth finally prevailed. Established French society was not to be predicated on an incontrovertible falsehood.

A comparison between the fate of the myth of the November criminals and the Dreyfus case suggests a difference between the two societies, a slight but telling difference in the mix of collective sanity and delusion. In both societies, truth and falsehood were contending for dominance; truth finally gained the advantage in the French society; falsehood, in the German one.

Even if the difference between the contending forces in French society were very slight, as they seem to have been, a comparison with Germany may be revealing in terms of collective emotion dynamics. It suggests that French society had enough collective self-esteem, i.e., *pride*, to acknowledge the fact of military defeat but that German society did not. To the extent that my analysis of these two cases is accurate, it suggests that collective acknowledgment of shame can have fateful consequences for whole nations.

Long-Term Implications for Reconciliation Between Nations

If the theory proposed here has any validity, it should have implications for progress toward global peace and security. Now I wish to explore several long-range and two immediate directions toward resolving world conflict.

How can groups involved in interminable conflicts extricate themselves? One implication of my discussion so far is that this is a difficult problem because the social and emotional causes lie buried far beneath the surface of consciousness. As has been indicated, if it is true that denial of interdependence and shame is deeply institutionalized in modern societies, these basic causes would be virtually invisible to most persons in the contending groups. These kinds of issues are not raised in even the best of the conventional approaches to international dispute resolution, such as Kriesberg (1992). One long-range direction suggested by earlier chapters is the need to reduce the high levels of secrecy and deception within and between nations that are a prominent feature of our civilization. Secrecy and deception cause and are caused by self-deception; all three phenomena are essential features of dysfunctional communication.

Chapter 4 suggested that deception between nations and self-deception within them, secret diplomacy, and terrorism were a crucial part of the path to World

War I. The parallels in the contemporary activities of our own government and that of other countries are obvious. In the Reagan and Bush administrations, and even more so in the then-Communist societies, these practices were not only institutionalized but also virtually sanctified. It may be important for social scientists and others to reassess the role of secrecy and lying in public and personal life. There is a strong current of opinion in modern social science that secrecy has constitutive social functions, even though there are now available powerful arguments to the contrary (see Chapter 4).

It is conceivable that in the long run help in this matter may come from an unexpected direction. A possible consequence of nuclear terror may be that nations will increasingly be required to allow open inspection in order to demonstrate that nuclear limitations are being followed. Perhaps this restricted issue could be enlarged by using it as a metaphor for a vast change that is needed in relationships between nations. A secure bond between parties requires that each allows itself to be known to the other and seeks to know the other.

In this context, a policy of openness, rather than of secrecy and restriction, could lead to the enhancement of the overall bonds between nations, not just to the reduction of nuclear insecurity. What may be needed as a step toward increased social solidarity in the world social system is not only surveillance but also increasing economic, technological, and cultural interchange between the now largely sequestered nations of the world.

This is not to say that increasing interchange necessarily leads to increasing cooperation. Currently, interchange may be leading more often to increasing competition and hostility (as in the strife related to immigration and guest workers in Europe). What has been established in family systems theory is that bonding has less to do with the volume of interchange and more with its quality, particularly its manner (Chapter 3). Usually the manner of a statement is at least as important as its content in perpetuating or easing tension and conflict.

Another long-term direction would be to encourage more open acceptance and expression of the emotions of pride and shame in both public and private arenas. Such a change might allow for more acknowledgment of human interdependence and less denial. If, as I have argued here, the denial of interdependence generates alienation and interminable conflict, how might this process be reversed at its roots? As already indicated, this is a profoundly difficult problem since shame is deeply denied in modern societies.

Public acknowledgment of shame followed by apology and restitution toward the victims might be an important step in this direction. In modern civilizations, it is rare but not unknown. Recently the U.S. government took such a step toward the Japanese-Americans who were unjustly interned during World War II. As Tavuchis pointed out, there have been gestures in this direction in Canada toward rectifying the vast injustice done to its native peoples, but full apology and reconciliation may be a long time coming.

In a similar context, after World War II the government of Western Germany established a program of financial restitution to the survivors of the Nazi genocide of the Jews. (My own aunt, who is French, was a beneficiary of this program; the German government acknowledged its responsibility for the death of my uncle.) Nevertheless, the government did not take, and still has not taken, sufficient symbolic steps toward apology.

One step in the right direction was Brandt's visit to the Jewish resistance monument in the Warsaw Ghetto during his chancellorship. His kneeling and weeping at the monument were spontaneous, but they were the kind of gesture required for forgiveness to occur. His gesture cost nothing, but it was probably worth at least as much as all the reparation money that West Germany paid. The current governments of Russia and other former Eastern bloc countries face a vast problem of this kind in acknowledging the crimes of Stalin's regime toward its own and other peoples.

The historical shame sequence that Elias (1978) uncovered in his study of manners suggests an approach to this difficult but important issue. He showed that the repression of shame has occurred so gradually and in such small increments, beginning more than five hundred years ago, that it has been all but invisible. Advice manuals at the beginning of the modern era were explicit verbal instructions from one adult to another regarding how to be a worthy person. Detailed instructions stated clearly the purpose of good manners: their practical advantages, and their moral one, i.e., showing *respect* toward others. For this reason there was little mystery about courtesy and good breeding.

Over the course of time, however, advice about elemental issues of decency in regard to courtesy, the body and personal appearance, and emotions evolved in a way that led to mystification and shame. In the modern era, basic socialization in these realms is between adults and children. Rather than small movements in the level of repression occurring gradually over the course of centuries, infants and children are rapidly socialized in only a few years. In this process, there is little detailed verbal explanation of exactly what respect is wanted and why it is wanted.

Modern etiquette manuals, a mode of adult socialization, give little advice in these key matters. Where advice is given, it is often abstract and vague. The implication is that a decent person already knows, a practice that reeks of embarrassment and repression. The modern socialization of both children and adults may automatically inculcate shame. Modernity is like a ship afloat on a river of shame. (For a recent and partially humorous attempt to begin rehabilitating shame as a legitimate human feeling, see Turner et al.'s description of a new holiday, "Blushing Monday," 1991.)

In this context there is a need for reducing shame levels in the socialization of children and adults at the most fundamental levels, in the family and in school. Before this can happen, however, it may be necessary to develop a new language, one that does not deny interdependence and emotion. For this reason building an alternative social science around the concept of human interdependence, and an alternative social psychology that speaks in the language of emotion, may be the most pressing problems for contemporary social science.

One of the difficulties in increasing interchange between nations is language differences. High-quality translation, which increases understanding rather than misunderstanding, requires great skill and knowledge of both cultures. If the nations of the world are to live together in increasing interdependence, it may be necessary to enhance the status of the professional translator and to increase the amount and quality of training available for this arduous task. In a brilliant compendium on translation, Steiner (1971) highlighted the difficulty and the importance of the translator's role.

Accurate translation requires part/whole reasoning skills: being able to deal with the smallest parts of a problem, the largest wholes, and the relationships between them (Mills, 1959; Scheff, 1990). Another profession that may be important for world peace is that of the mediator, which also requires these skills. Although a relatively new occupation, it might make contributions to resolving collective conflicts. It is the only profession at present devoted solely to peacemaking. It might be necessary to establish a new discipline within universities for this purpose so that research and professional training could proceed apace.

At present most persons serving as mediators have been trained as either lawyers or psychotherapists. Although both types of training can provide mediation skills, they also both have severe limitations. In terms of my argument here, the most crucial may be the undermining of part/whole thinking.

Current legal and psychotherapy training may reduce, rather than increase, this ability. Future lawyers and psychotherapists often learn to focus on one part of the larger system, their client, disregarding the interests of the whole. In family courts mediators report that the lawyers and psychotherapists representing clients in a case often increase conflict rather than reduce it. Perhaps establishing unique, thorough, and high-prestige training for translators and for mediators would produce more effective peacemakers.

Directions for Immediate Change

The ideas just advanced about needed changes toward peace concerned long-range goals. I now address two ideas concerning first steps: a new approach toward mediation and the problem of lustration. The first idea involves a change in the type of mediation used in large-scale negotiations of conflict. My reading of newspaper reports and viewing of the televised proceedings of the Madrid conference between Arab countries and Israel left me with a strong impression of both intentional and inadvertent insult and innuendo by many of the participants. These indications were flagrant in the speeches of some of the Israeli and Arab speakers.

Mediation Between Nations

The kind of mediation I propose would follow from the theory described in this book rather than the contemporary practice of mediation and arbitration between disputing nations. Too often current attempts are as trapped in topics as the disputants are, ignoring relational issues and emotions. Also needing discussion is the group dynamics of the mediation efforts.

Peacemaking between nations in current practice typically involves largely public meetings between two or more opposing groups. In this context, group dynamics and the very architecture of the meeting rooms seem to foster bimodal alienation. The broadcasts of the Madrid conference that I saw showed the Arab and Israeli representatives denouncing each other to visibly large audiences. The speakers' awareness of TV cameras added an even larger audience to their perception of the situation.

Under such circumstances, there is little room for creative ideas and the repair of damaged bonds. Speakers feel constrained to reaffirm their loyalty within their own group and their isolation and hostility toward the other group. To allow room for maneuver, a radically different format may be necessary.

One possibility would be to arrange for as many one-on-one private encounters as the disputants would allow. Formal meetings would always be held in the presence of a mediator with substantial experience in dealing with persons in crisis, as in divorce and custody mediation and other forms of high-conflict disputes. Perhaps the the most productive form of single encounters would be between opposite numbers: The leading representatives of each group meeting, the next highest, and so on. Being in the same position might help establish a minimal amount of identification between the opponents, which could be the first step toward building a bond. Private meetings of this type might also lead to creative thoughts about resolving the conflict.

Encouraging many informal one-on-one encounters might also be important. In scientific conferences, significant interchanges often occur over meals or on social occasions. Even in these settings, however, the presence of mediators might help set the tone of dialogue away from dispute and toward problemsolving.

Large groups would also be important, especially at the beginning and end of the meetings. The format of these large meetings could be carefully designed by mediators to encourage conciliation. Perhaps the plenary session would revolve around a talk by an independent expert designed to introduce new frames of reference into the conflict. Other initial group meetings might be limited to statements of the costs of the conflict to each side. As in current mediation practice, the later group meetings would be organized to emphasize the areas of agreement and the gains toward conciliation made by the conference. The main focus of the kind of mediation outlined here would not be on the topics of the dispute but on the repair of damage to the social and emotional bond between the disputants. To flesh out these abstract ideas, I use the crisis set off by the Austrian ultimatum to Serbia in July 1914 (already mentioned in Chapter 4) as a hypothetical.

After the assassination of Archduke Ferdinand, the Austrian government made the following demands:

1. The suppression of any publication inciting hatred of Austria-Hungary.
2. The dissolution of Narodna Odbrana and all other propaganda societies, and the taking of necessary measures to prevent the dissolved societies from continuing their activities under another name and form.
3. The elimination from Serbian schools of hate propaganda against Austria-Hungary.
4. The removal from the Serbian army and bureaucracy of officers and officials guilty of propaganda against Austria-Hungary.
5. The acceptance of the collaboration in Serbia of Austrian officials in the suppression of the subversive movement.
6. The arrest of the accessories to the murder plot of June 28, and the participation of Austrian officials in the investigation of the assassination.
7. The arrest of Major Voja Tankosich and Milan Ciganovich.
8. The suppression of the illegal traffic of arms and explosives from Serbia into Austria, and the punishment of the frontier officials who had helped the murderers to cross into Austria.
9. An explanation of the "unjustifiable utterances of high Serbian officials both in Serbia and abroad" who had, in interviews since June 28, expressed hostility to Austria-Hungary.
10. The notification of the Austrian government, without delay, of the measures taken. (Goodspeed, 1977, pp. 125–126)

Suppose that in an attempt to avoid war, mediation not only between Serbia and Austria but also between the Allies and the Central Powers had been held. If such mediation had followed current practice, it would have separated out the three items directly connected with the assassination (6, 7, and 8) for immediate attention. The mediator would have reasoned that by putting the other items on hold, the disputants might be able to reach some quick agreements. The next step would probably have been to separate the more tendentious elements out of these three items, such as the requirement that Austria participate directly in the investigation (item 6). Finally, the mediator would have tried to reframe the more general demands in a way that both sides might find acceptable.

One obvious consideration here is that in this particular case, reasonable steps like these would have been doomed to failure because any serious investigation of the assassination would have ultimately shown the involvment not only of the Serbian government but also of Russia, as indicated in Chapter 4. This objection does not undercut the main purpose of my proposal, however. If the other European nations had insisted on thirty days of nonbinding mediation between the two countries, both would probably have agreed, if only for the sake of appearances. A thirty-day period would have allowed tempers to cool. Perhaps the crowds in the streets of the major cities of Europe would have thinned, easing the pressure on the governments for war. Students of collective behavior (see

Shibutani, 1990, for example) have argued that highly mobilized crowds are in a state of collective delusion, which makes them irrational. A cooling off period allows for reasoned argument, which can undercut the emotions that fuel the urge to fight.

The style of mediation that I propose would be a further step in this direction. The feature of the Austrian ultimatum that current mediation practice might ignore is that its tone was insulting to the point of humiliation. Most of the items impled a violation of Serbian sovereignty by Austrian officials if the demands were accepted or even if they were taken as worthy of serious consideration. Even more insulting was the imperiousness of the demand that a complete answer be forthcoming within forty-eight hours. (The Serbians met this demand, but only by rejecting, in effect, virtually all the others.)

The insult to Serbia was not the most important consequence of the ultimatum. More important for the peace of the world was that the demands were a flagrant affront to Russia since the Russian government saw itself as Serbia's protector; and it was seen as such by all the other nations. Since the Russians were insecure about their place among the powerful nations, with considerable justification, the Austrian ultimatum generated intense pressure in the Russian government for retaliation at whatever cost.

A skillful mediation would have allowed Serbian and Russian representatives to express their sense of insult and humilation. It is conceivable that such expressions might have led to division between the war and peace factions in Austria-Hungary and Germany. For example, in this episode the prime minister of Hungary, Tiza, was extremely forceful in opposing war against Serbia. If the peace faction had prevailed, a new ultimatum from Austria, reworded to tone down the insult, could have slowed down the spiral of conflict. The hypothetical exchange would have been an example of acknowledgment of hidden shame and anger on both sides. It would not have guaranteed a different outcome, but it would have been worth a try.

The Problem of Lustration

The second direction concerns the process of lustration, rituals of collective purification. In present usage, the most common of these rituals are show trials, like those going on in contemporary Eastern Europe. Show trials do not seem to decrease division but often to increase it, as seems to have occurred in the trials in the former Czechoslovakia. To end this chapter, I discuss a possible alternative.

Braithwaite's (1989) work on reintegrative shaming suggested a framework for exploring the process of lustration. Controls of crime, Braithwaite proposed, can be classified as one of two types: stigmatization and reintegrative shaming. The first type results in separation between the offender and society; most frequently, offenders are punished by being imprisoned. Although stigmatization is a highly elaborated ritual of separation involving denunciation and the removal of civil rights, there is usually no equally prominent ritual of reinstatement. Once imprisoned, the offender runs the risk of being unable to reestablish self as an accepted member of society.

In the second type of control, the offender is punished by public denunciation and shaming. Unlike stigmatization, the punishment process is always followed by a highly visible ceremony of reacceptance. To become qualified for this ceremony, however, the offender is usually required to complete remedial actions, such as restitution, community work, confession, and apology.

Show trials virtually always involve punishment of the stigmatizing kind. As an example, I once again refer to the case of Speer. Although the Nuremburg judges spared his life, he was imprisoned for twenty-one years. This punishment seemed to have not greatly changed his basic perspective. Also the trial and imprisonment may have missed an opportunity for lustration, for a ritual of collective purification from the Nazi era. How could such an objective have been accomplished?

The following outline is only a preliminary sketch of one direction that might have been taken. In the first place, the trial of the Nazi war criminals would have been conducted, not by the Allies, but by the new German government in Bonn. The trial would have been an opportunity both for lustration and for a demonstration to the world that a fundamental change had taken place in Germany.

For effective lustration to have taken place, the punishment should have been the reintegrative shaming process just described rather than death or lengthy imprisonment. Given the enormity of the crimes committed, however, the remedial actions required of the offenders would have had to have been of great scope and intensity if a sense of justice was to prevail.

The emphasis on repairing bonds in this book leads to the idea that the offenders might have been sentenced to some type of victim confrontation on a scale commensurate with the scope of their crimes. Suppose that the court had arranged for each offender to learn about the effects of the Nazi program directly from its victims and their surviving kin. The offender's working day during his period of imprisonment might have been spent listening to victim and kin's stories of their suffering.

The persons testifying would have been treated by the prison as visitors. For the offender's protection, they would have spoken to him through a glass partition. An officer of the court would have been present to advise the visitors to tell their story without verbal abuse of the prisoner. After hearing several hundred such stories, perhaps most of the offenders might have broken down and wept.

It is possible that this kind of confrontation would have provided a corrective experience for the offenders, creating a bond between them and their victims where none had existed before. For a man like Speer, this process could have occurred in only a few years. He might then have been able to make a real apology, one that was not hollow and cerebral but deeply felt. (In a personal communication, John Braithwaite suggested that a more carefully controlled format of confrontation might be needed to avoid the possibility of further hardening the offenders. Perhaps offenders might be allowed to choose to help some of the families they meet, to become active in their lives in a way that might build a social bond.)

A genuine apology from Speer might have had two important effects. For his judges, it could have served as a signal for his qualification for reintegration into society. Speer was a brilliant man whose skills might have helped to rebuild German society. If his apology had been broadcast publicly, it could also have served as a denunciation of the Nazi past to those in Germany who still clung to it. From this point of view, the executions and imprisonment that resulted from the Nuremburg trials wasted a valuable opportunity for collective healing within Germany and for reconciliation between it and other nations.

Similarly, an effective process of lustration in the period 1918–1933 might have helped prevent World War II. Another hypothetical can be drawn from the Russian case. The execution of the czar and his family set a precedent for violence in the Communist government and passed up the opportunity for a public denunciation of the old regime and the reintegration of its leaders.

A final example is suggested by the Chinese Communist experience. The Chinese initially used effective forms of lustration at local levels, such as their "speak bitterness" meetings. Such meetings mobilized the peasants and helped integrate them into a new society. Apparently, however, these forms became corrupt after the Communists took power. Like most of the other ideas in this book, developing a theory and practice of effective mediation between nations and lustration within them will require considerably more discussion and exploration.

References

Barres, M. 1905. *Au service de l'Allemagne*. Paris: A. Fayard.

_____. 1909. *Colette Baudoche*. Paris: Juven.

Boisdeffre, P. 1962. *Maurice Barres*. Paris: University Editions.

Bok, S. 1978. *Lying*. New York: Vintage Books.

_____. 1983. *Secrets*. New York: Vintage Books.

Braithwaite, J. 1989. *Crime, Shame, and Reintegration*. Cambridge: Cambridge Univ. Press.

Deroulede, P. 1872. *Chants du soldat*. Paris: Calman Levy.

_____. 1896. *Poesies militare*. Paris: Calman Levy.

Doty, C. S. 1976. *From Cultural Rebellion to Revolution*. Columbus: Ohio State Univ. Press

Drumont, E. 1886. *La France Juive*. Paris: Flammarion.

Ekman, P., and W. Friesen. 1978. *Facial Action Coding System*. Palo Alto, CA: Consulting Psychologists Press.

Elias, N. 1978. *The History of Manners*. New York: Vintage Books.

_____. 1989. *The Individual and the Group*. London: Basil Blackwell.

Freud, S. [1896] 1961. *Studies of Hysteria*. New York: Avon Books.

Gaylin, W. 1984. *The Rage Within*. New York: Simon and Schuster.

Goffman, E. 1967. *Interaction Ritual*. Garden City, NY: Anchor Books.

_____. 1971. *Relations in Public.* New York: Harper.

Goodspeed, D. J. 1977. *The German Wars: 1914–1915.* Boston: Houghton Mifflin.

Gottschalk, L., C. Wingert, and G. Gleser. 1969. *Manual of Instruction for Using the Gottschalk-Gleser Content Analysis Scales.* Berkeley and Los Angeles: Univ. of California Press

Hitler, A. [1927] 1943. *Mein Kampf.* Boston: Houghton Mifflin..

Izard, C. 1979. *The Maximally Discriminant Facial Movement Coding System.* Newark: Univ. of Delaware.

Kennan, G. 1984. *The Fateful Alliance: France, Russia, and the Coming of the First World War.* New York: Pantheon Books.

Kriesberg, L. 1992. *International Conflict Resolution.* New Haven: Yale Univ. Press.

Lewis, H. B. 1971. *Shame and Guilt in Neurosis.* New York: International Universities Press.

Lynd, H. 1958. *On Shame and the Search for Identity.* New York: Harcourt.

Mills, C. W. 1959. *The Sociological Imagination.* New York: Oxford Univ. Press.

Mitscherlich, A., and M. Mitscherlich. 1975. *The Inability to Mourn.* New York: Grove Press.

Retzinger, S. M. 1991. *Violent Emotions: Shame and Rage in Marital Quarrels.* Newbury Park, CA: Sage.

Rutkoff, P. M. 1981. *Revanche and Revision.* Athens: Ohio Univ. Press.

Scheff, T. J. 1979. *Catharsis in Healing, Ritual, and Drama.* Berkeley and Los Angeles: Univ. of California Press.

_____. 1990. *Microsociology: Discourse, Emotion, and Social Structure.* Chicago: Univ. of Chicago Press.

Scheff, T. J., and S. M. Retzinger. 1991. *Emotion and Violence: Shame and Rage in Destructive Conflicts.* Lexington, MA: Lexington Books.

Shibutani, T. 1990. *Social Processes.* Berkeley and Los Angeles: Univ. of California Press.

Sontag, R. 1933. *European Diplomatic History.* New York: Appleton-Century.

Speer, A. 1970. *Inside the Third Reich.* New York: Macmillan.

Steiner, G. 1971. *After Babel.* New York: Oxford Univ. Press.

Tavuchis, N. 1991. *Mea Culpa: A Sociology of Apology and Reconciliation.* Stanford: Stanford U.niv Press

Turner, F. 1991. "Blushing Monday: A Day Set Aside to Revel in Shame." *Harper's Magazine* (August):40–45.

Volkan, V. 1988. *The Need to Have Enemies and Allies.* Northvale, NJ: Jason Aronson.

Waite, R. 1977. *The Psychopathic God: Adolf Hitler.* New York: Basic Books.

Weber, E. 1968. *The Nationalist Revival in France, 1905–1914.* Berkeley and Los Angeles: Univ. of California Press.

Appendix:
Cues for Shame and Anger

Verbal Markers

SHAME:
Alienated: rejected, dumped, deserted, rebuff, abandoned, estranged, isolated, separate, alone, disconnected, disassociated, detached, withdrawn, inhibited, distant, remote, split, divorced, polarized.

Confused: stunned, dazed, blank, empty, hollow, spaced, giddy, lost, vapid, hesitant, aloof.

Ridiculous: foolish, silly, funny, absurd, idiotic, asinine, simple-minded, stupid, curious, weird, bizarre, odd, peculiar, strange, different, stupid.

Inadequate: helpless, powerless, defenseless, weak, insecure, uncertain, shy, deficient, worse off, small, failed, ineffectual, inferior, unworthy, worthless, flawed, trivial, meaningless, insufficient, unsure, dependent, exposed, inadequate, incapable, vulnerable, unable, inept, unfit, impotent, oppressed.

Uncomfortable: restless, fidgety, jittery, tense, anxious, nervous, uneasy, antsy, jumpy, hyperactive.

Hurt: offended, upset, wounded, injured, tortured, ruined, sensitive, sore spot, buttons pushed, dejected, intimidated, defeated.

ANGER: cranky, cross, hot-tempered, ireful, quick-tempered, short-fused, enraged, fuming, agitated, furious, irritable, incensed, indignant, irate, annoyed, mad, pissed, pissed off, teed-off, upset, furious, aggravated, bothered, resentful, bitter, spiteful, grudging (the last four words imply shame-rage compounds).

Other Verbal Markers

SHAME: mitigation (to make appear less severe or painful); oblique, suppressed reference, e.g., "they," "it," "you"; vagueness; denial; defensiveness; verbal withdrawal (lack of response); indifference (acting "cool" in an emotionally arousing context).

ANGER: interruption; challenge; sarcasm; blame.

SHAME-RAGE: temporal expansion/condensation or generalization ("You always ..."; "You never ..."); triangulation (bringing up an irrelevant third party or object).

Paralinguistic Markers

SHAME: vocal withdrawal/hiding behaviors, disorganization of thought: oversoft irregular rhythm; hesitation; self-interruption (censorship); filled pauses (-uh-); long pauses; silences; stammering; fragmented speech; rapid speech; condensed words; mumbling; breathiness; incoherence (lax articulation); laughed words; monotone.

ANGER: staccato (distinct breaks between successive tones); loudness; heavy stress on certain words; singsong pattern (ridicule); straining; harsh voice qualifiers.

SHAME-RAGE: whine; glottalization (rasp or buzz); choking; tempo up/down; pitch up/down.

Visual Markers

SHAME: (1) hiding behavior: (a) the hand covering all or parts of the face; (b) gaze aversion, eyes lowered or averted. (2) blushing. (3) control: (a) turning in, biting, or licking the lips, biting the tongue; (b) forehead wrinkled vertically or transversely; (c) false smiling (Ekman and Friesen, 1982); or other masking behaviors.

ANGER: (1) brows lowered and drawn together, vertical lines appearing between them. (2) eyelids narrowed and tense in a hard fixed stare and maybe with a bulging appearance. (3) lips pressed together, the corners straight or down or open but tense and square. (4) hard direct glaring. (5) leaning forward toward other in challenging stance. (6) clenched fists, waving fists, hitting motions.

Like all human expressions (including words), the meaning of these markers is context related; that is, their relevance depends on the relationship between self and other. Look for constellation of markers in context; the more markers there are from each category, the stronger the evidence is.

SOURCE: Suzanne Retzinger, *Violent Emotions: Shame and Rage in Marital Quarrels* (Newbury Park, CA: Sage, 1991). Copyright © 1991 by Sage Publications, Inc. Reprinted by permission of Sage Publications, Inc.

REFERENCE: P. Ekman, and W. Friesen. 1982. "Felt, False, and Miserable Smiles." *Journal of Nonverbal Behavior* 6: 238–252.

Index